# Writing Public Policy

*A Practical Guide to Communicating
in the Policy Making Process*

THIRD EDITION

## Catherine F. Smith

*East Carolina University*
*University of North Carolina at Chapel Hill*

**OXFORD**
UNIVERSITY PRESS

Oxford University Press is a department of the University of Oxford.
It furthers the University's objective of excellence in research,
scholarship, and education by publishing worldwide.

Oxford New York
Auckland Cape Town Dar es Salaam Hong Kong Karachi
Kuala Lumpur Madrid Melbourne Mexico City Nairobi
New Delhi Shanghai Taipei Toronto

With offices in
Argentina Austria Brazil Chile Czech Republic France Greece
Guatemala Hungary Italy Japan Poland Portugal Singapore
South Korea Switzerland Thailand Turkey Ukraine Vietnam

Copyright © 2013, 2010, 2005 by Oxford University Press.

Published by Oxford University Press.
198 Madison Avenue, New York, New York 10016
http://www.oup.com

**Library of Congress Cataloging-in-Publication Data**

Smith, Catherine F. (Catherine Findley), 1942–
Writing public policy: a practical guide to communicating in the policy-making
process / Catherine F. Smith.—3rd ed.
    p. cm.
Includes index.
ISBN 978-0-19-993392-1 (pbk.)
1. Communication in public administration.   2. Written communication.
I. Title.
JF1525.C59S64 2012
320.6—dc23                                                    2012018885

Printing number:  9 8 7 6 5 4 3 2 1

Printed in the United States of America
on acid-free paper

*To my family of exemplars in public and community service—*

*John (again), Ian, Lauren*
*Jimmy, Floride, Marian, David*

# Brief Contents

# Contents

# Who Is the Intended Audience?

Primarily, this book addresses undergraduate and graduate students of public policy, political science, public administration, public discourse, writing, and communication, along with their teachers.

Entry-level professionals in government, management, nonprofit organization, politics, public policy, public relations, public affairs, public administration, social work, public safety, or public health will find the guide useful.

Active citizens who are engaged in community issues, politics, or government, or those who serve in civic organizations, will find the guide useful, too.

## Special Features of This Book

You will find the following learning strategies here:

- case illustrations and scenarios showing the policymaking process in cultural context
- writing samples by professionals, students, and citizens participating in government and nonprofit organizations
- commentary to show how the writing samples apply communication principles, perform thinking or communication tasks, and meet expected standards
- a general method for communicating, with checklists for planning, producing, and assessing documents
- specific instructions for selected document types

Every scenario and sample is taken from actual policy work in governmental, organizational, or educational settings. Most represent the work of professionals in government or nonprofit organizations; some represent the work of students in classroom simulations. A few represent both. Students who, at the time of writing, were also government professionals or organization interns produced communications that crossed over into actual use in a policy process. The samples are just that, examples, not models. They are work products, presented as written. (When requested, names have been removed. Most samples have been condensed, owing to space limitations.)

The cases, scenarios, and samples provide a realistic and multifaceted overview of the policy process and its written products without oversimplification. This guide's immersion approach to developing know-how assumes that broad exposure develops a feel for the territory and a sense of its predictability as well as variability. Consequently, a singular case of policy making to which all the scenarios and samples relate is not presented here. Instead, you will find exemplification drawn from multiple policy processes. Coherence is provided by sustained topics such as health, safety, and fairness that turn up like themes in a novel. Coherence also comes from the presence of exemplars. Some are communicators who turn up in several chapters to show a policy actor writing to progress through phases of a policy process. These exemplars' documents turn up in several chapters to illustrate varied communication practices or to show a policy actor reusing information for different purposes or audiences across contexts.

Given the real demands of public policy making, this guide assumes that communicators in the process need both general know-how and specific skills. So, in addition to description of the work, a general method of rhetorical and strategic planning is provided here, along with detailed task-by-task instructions for commonly used genres or types of communication. Together the method and instructions provide a disciplined approach to writing and speaking under typical working conditions of public policy activity.

Limits of this guide should be noted. First, the emphasis is on communicating in, or with, government. The emphasis is justifiable because government makes most public policy and because people know too little about what government does and does not do. Other actors are certainly involved. Here, they are included as influences on the process as it occurs in the governmental framework. For example, while it is true that large-scale corporate or religious or educational institutions indirectly make public policy by the effect of their independent actions, those actors are addressed here as influences on governmental policy making.

Second, writing samples and commentary refer only to U.S. domestic policy communication. Global and international policy communications are outside the scope of this short guide, except for impacts of the global Internet and international "plain English."

# Introduction:
# How to Use This Book

To benefit from this book, you do not need prior experience as a student of public policy, as an intern in government, as a student in community-based learning, as an activist in campus or community affairs, or as a volunteer in a nonprofit organization. Any such experience will be very helpful, and you can draw on it often as you use this book. But it is not required. Experience or training in professional or business or administrative communication will be helpful, too, but it is not required.

You will find this book useful if

- you are majoring in the social sciences or humanities to prepare for a career in politics, government, public relations, law, public policy, journalism, social work, or public health

- you are (or might in the future be) an intern in government, in a think tank, or in a nongovernmental organization concerned with public affairs

- you are preparing to enter (or you are already practicing in) a publicly regulated industry or business

- you have (or seek) a job as a communications aide in government or a political action organization

- you have (or seek) a job as a public policy/public relations director in a nonprofit organization or as a public affairs liaison in a corporation, trade organization, professional association, or community service agency

- you are a writer, and you write about public affairs
- you are concerned about a local, national, or world problem, and you want to do something about it
- you want or are asked to comment publicly on a controversy and you do not feel you have the authority or knowledge or skill to do that

## How Should You Use This Book?

It is a manual of practice, or guide, so you can use it whenever you have a wish or face a demand to enter a public forum or to participate in a public policymaking process. Here's the intended model of use, whether you are a student, professional, or active citizen. You bring experience, knowledge, willingness to learn, persistence, and a motivating topic of concern. In the book, first read the foundational chapters 1 and 2. Before you write (or speak) on the topic of concern, answer general questions about the policy process (General Method, chapter 2) to make yourself aware of the cultural context and the rhetorical situation of your intended communication, and to plan the product. Then follow the specific instructions (chapters 3 through 10) to compose the product with awareness of the context and your plan. If your product will appear on the Web, review the guidance on networked policy writing (Appendix). After you compose, use the checklists of expected qualities in policy communications (chapter 2) to assess the product. Revise it as necessary before communicating it.

Do you need all of the book or only parts? That depends on your intentions and circumstances. The chapters build on one another, but they can be used separately. If you are a student in a policy writing course, you might use this entire book. Start with a topic of concern; then compose the necessary communications to "work" the topic through a typical policy process. The benefits of using the entire book are that writers gain increased knowledge of a topic and an overview of the policy making process while developing competencies in an integrated set of communication practices. For a collaborative project, writers might divide up the communication responsibilities and designate individuals to produce particular documents or presentations using relevant chapters. That way, individuals gain practical experience with one or more of the types of communication while the group collectively gains an overview of the process.

If you are learning independently to meet a particular demand, use the chapters that fit the demand.

If you feel intimidated because you don't know enough about a subject or about policy making or about policy writing, do not worry. Your knowledge will grow as you practice the communications this book teaches. (This encouragement comes to you directly from evaluations by students who used this book.)

Tip: Several chapters (3, 5, and 9) anticipate research and communication tasks that may be given without much warning to interns, volunteers, and professionals new on the job, ready or not. If that happens to you, after first reviewing chapter 2 on communicating in context, you might find chapter 3 on problem definition, chapter 5 on legislative records research, and chapter 9 on witness testimony particularly helpful.

Pay special attention to the features of this book that are intended to help you learn. Overall, this text provides a general method for communicating and includes checklists for planning, producing, and assessing documents. In each chapter, you will find instructions for a specific genre or type of communication. Writing samples by professionals, students, and citizens in government or nonprofit organizations are presented throughout the book. Scenarios show the samples in context. Accompanying commentary shows how the samples apply communication principles, meet expected standards, and do policy work.

# List of Writing Samples

# CHAPTER 1

# Public Policy Making

## Key Concepts

- problem solving process
- governmental framework
- pluralism

This guide to communication is informed by the idea of public policy making as a democratic process of solving problems. This chapter frames the process from the perspective of communication and offers two illustrative cases. Other ways to think about public policy making are found in suggested readings at the end of this chapter.

Public policy exists to solve problems affecting people in society (Coplin and O'Leary 1998, p. 2). Making public policy means deciding what is and is not a problem, choosing which problems to solve, and deciding on solutions. The process occurs in a political context of pluralism. Problems are conceived and defined differently by variously interested actors. Solutions are achieved through mutual adjustment and adaptation of interests. Decision often demands compromise and reflects institutional constraints. The framework for decision is governmental.

## Case 1: Milk Labeling

On October 24, 2007, Pennsylvania announced a new standard of food safety aimed to prevent "mislabeling" of food products, especially "misleading" labels. That's *public policy*, a standing decision by government. An administrative agency, the state's department of agriculture, targeted dairy food as the problem. Specifically, milk produced or sold in Pennsylvania could not be labeled as "hormone-free." Labels could not say that milk came from cows not treated with "artificial growth hormone" or with "rBGH" or "rBST," common acronyms for recombinant bovine somatotropine growth hormone.

Politics influenced the decision. Arguably, the agency's decision to target milk labeling favored one set of stakeholders, the maker of rBST and dairy farmers who use it. That coalition had long argued that milk labels saying "no artificial growth hormone" or similar language harmed sales of their products by implying that milk from cows treated with rBST is unsafe. They cited Federal Drug Administration (FDA) approval for rBST use and scientific evidence of its safety. The state agriculture secretary agreed.

The agency's decision was immediately controversial in Pennsylvania and elsewhere. News and reaction spread through newspaper, telephone, e-mail, blogs, and chat outlets. Dairy farmers who did not use rBST and who wanted to say they did not on milk labels organized rapidly to oppose the ban. Advocates for sustainable agriculture joined these farmers in coalition. They counterargued that the science on rBST's safety is inconclusive, that farmers have a right to inform consumers about their product, and that consumers have the right to make informed choices. Plans for litigation against the state were announced. In parallel action, farmers who did use rBST organized to react in coalition with other advocacy groups in support of the ban.

In mid-November, Pennsylvania's governor postponed the ban, and then cancelled it. On January 17, 2008, the governor along with the secretary of agriculture announced two policy changes, a revised standard for dairy product labeling and new procedures for oversight of labeling claims. Under rule revisions, labels are permitted to claim that milk came from cows not treated with rBST along with a disclaimer as to its potential for health risk. Dairy food processors are required to verify label claims by having dairy farmers sign affidavits regarding production methods. That's *policy making* in institutional democracy.

This snapshot captures the basics. For a more complete view of this case, read participants' own communications. They reveal dimensions of debate, and they illustrate a typical mix of policy writing styles. Extracts selected from key participants' statements are presented here. To read the full text of these and related communications, go to the source cited. The following extracts start with the state's initial announcement and follow the story as it developed.

## Government Chooses a Problem

### Memorandum

*To:* Agriculture and Food Labeling Stakeholders

*From:* Secretary Dennis C. Wolff

*Subject:* Product Label Review Update

*Date:* October 23, 2007

The Pennsylvania Department of Agriculture (PDA) is increasingly being made aware of concerns from consumers, farmers, and public policy makers regarding mislabeled food products. These include concerns as to whether label claims are accurate and verifiable, and whether label claims are misleading.

  For example, concerns have been raised that some labels are misleading consumers by promoting what is *not* in the product....I recently called upon help from a group of dietitians, consumer advocates, and food industry representatives on current issues relating to food labeling by establishing the Food Labeling Advisory Committee...While widespread food labeling concerns existed, the Committee recommendation is to begin by addressing dairy labeling improprieties. This is a logical starting point, in that PDA has current legal responsibility to review certain milk and dairy product labels before they are used in commerce.

## Local and National Media Disseminate the News and Opinion

### "Milk-Labeling and Marketing Integrity"
By Hon. Dennis C. Wolff, Pennsylvania Secretary of Agriculture, *Lancaster Farming,* November 3, 2007

Consumers rely upon the labeling of a product when deciding what to buy for their families. Recently, concern has risen over the way milk products are labeled and the Department of Agriculture has taken action to help consumers make informed decisions about what to buy and to feed their families.

Some labels mislead by promoting what is not in the product, a practice called absence labeling. This marketing strategy is confusing and implies a safe versus not safe product.

...

I take issue with the fact that companies use false food labeling tactics to gain a market advantage.... Ultimately, we are seeking a solution to the labeling issue that will benefit those who produce Pennsylvania's food and those who consume it.

### "Consumers Won't Know What They're Missing"

By Andrew Martin, The Feed, NYTimes.com, November 11, 2007 http://www.nytimes.com/2007/11/11/business/11feed.html?_r=2& oref=slogin&oref=slogin

The Pennsylvania Department of Agriculture has decided that consumers are too dim to make their own shopping decisions. Agriculture officials in Ohio are contemplating a similar decision....

## Dairy Farmers React to Oppose the Ban

Opinion by Todd Rutter, dairy farmer, president of Rutter's Dairy in York, Pennsylvania. *Harrisburg Patriot News*, November 9, 2007. Quoted in Sherry Bunting, "Milk Label Issue Comes to a Boil in Pennsylvania," *Farmshine*, November 16, 2007; reprinted in Consumer Attitudes About Biotechnology, Science & Education, rbST Public Discussion, Penn State Dairy and Animal Science Blogs, Terry Etherton Blog on Biotechnology. http://blogs.das.psu.edu/tetherton/2007/11/17/ milk-label-issue-comes-to-a-boil-in-pennsylvania/

...The state's untenable position has only emboldened Rutter's in this regard, prompting us to plan a series of very public activities designed to educate the community and our customers about artificial growth hormones and our strong stance against their use in our milk production, not to mention our right to say so on our labels.

In the next couple of weeks, we will be running full-page newspaper ads, handing out more than 100,000 information cards through Rutter's Farm Stores, posting content at http://www.rutters.com, and, on Nov. 13, hand-delivering letters to every member of the Pennsylvania General Assembly. Of course, we're also pursuing all legal avenues available to us to protect our right to provide consumer information.

## Dairy Farmers React to Support the Ban

Opinion by Daniel Brandt, dairy farmer, Annville, Pennsylvania; PA Holstein Association State Director; Lebanon County Farm Bureau Director, November 17, 2007 at 12:16 pm. Filed under Consumer Attitudes About Biotechnology, Science & Education, rbST Public Discussion, Penn State Dairy and Animal Science Blogs, Terry Etherton Blog on Biotechnology. http://blogs.das.psu.edu/tetherton/2007/11/17/rutter-hormone-stutter/

In Todd Rutter's little rant in the November 9th *Harrisburg Patriot News*, it is shameful that he had no scientific documents to back up his claims....He does nothing to promote milk for what it is and the unprecedented benefits of drinking milk....

## Advocates Opposing the Ban Reframe the Debate

### "Time to Do the Right Thing with Food Labeling"
E-mail action alert, November 11, 2007, by Brian Snyder, Executive Director, Pennsylvania Association for Sustainable Agriculture, http://pasafarming.org; Leslie Zuck, Executive Director, Pennsylvania Certified Organic, http://www.paorganic.org; Timothy LaSalle, CEO, The Rodale Institute, http://www.rodaleinstitute.org

On its face, the recent decision by the Pennsylvania Department of Agriculture to conduct a crackdown on what it considers to be false or misleading claims on dairy product labels may seem to be in everyone's best interest....The essential question to ask is "What's really in everyone's best interest over the long term?"...The whole labeling controversy itself is only a sideshow to the real issues involved here, which have more to do with ethics and the industry-perceived need for the use of performance enhancing drugs in livestock production....The use of artificial growth hormones (rBST or rBGH) is certainly not the only example of such drugs being used on farms today. In fact, the majority of antibiotics sold in America are actually used in livestock production as growth promoting agents, not as treatment for disease in humans or animals as many uninformed, potentially confused consumers might assume.

...By all means, it makes perfect sense to employ the "precautionary principle" when research on any aspect of food production is not conclusive—in doing so, the countries of Canada, Australia, New Zealand, Japan and all 25 members of the European Union have already banned the use of rBST/rBHG in the production of milk.

So what's so wrong if an individual farmer or group of them working together wishes to advertise, even on a label, the choice made not to use such drugs at all, or at least not unless clinically indicated? While we are so busy debating when and how it is proper to put an absence claim on food labels, when do we get to consider the value of being completely forthcoming with consumers and letting them make informed choices?

## Expert Comments

### "rBST Certified Milk: A Story of Smoke and Mirrors"

By Terry Etherton, Distinguished Professor of Animal Nutrition and Head of the Department of Dairy and Animal Science, The Pennsylvania State University, October 3, 2006 at 4:23 pm. Filed under Agricultural Biotechnology, The Food System, rbST Public Discussion Penn State Dairy and Animal Science Blogs, Terry Etherton Blog on Biotechnology. http://blogs.das.psu.edu/tetherton/2006/10/03/rbst-certified-free-milk-a-story-of-smoke-and-mirrors/

The *Boston Globe* ran a story on Sept. 25th on the decision by H.P. Hood and Dean Foods to switch New England milk processing plants to "rbST-free" milk. In this story, a spokesperson for Dean Foods said, "Even though conventional milk is completely safe and...recombinant bovine somatotropin (rbST) is completely safe, some people don't feel comfortable with it"...There's little doubt that consumers who have no understanding are easily gulled by such labels...."If the future of our industry is based on marketing tactics that try to sway consumers with 'good milk' versus 'bad milk' messages, we are all in trouble," Kevin Holloway, President of Monsanto Dairy, told a group of dairy producers at a September 13th meeting in Washington D.C....

The reality I have observed is that it is easy to scare the public in a 30-second media message. It is impossible to give them a sound scientific understanding about the benefits of biotechnology in the barnyard in 30 seconds...One can ask, who wins? Junk science by a knockout...

## Government Revises the Policy

### "Governor Rendell says Consumers Can Have Greater Confidence in Milk Labels"

Office of the Governor, Commonwealth of Pennsylvania, Press Release, November 17, 2007

Governor Edward G. Rendell today announced that labels informing customers the milk they intend to buy is produced without rBST...can continue to be used...under new guidelines for accountability. "The public has a right to complete information about how the milk they buy is produced," said Governor Rendell.

## Government Promulgates a New Ruling

William Chirdon, Bureau Director, Commonwealth of Pennsylvania, Department of Agriculture, Bureau of Food Safety and Laboratory Services.

Dear Fluid Milk Permit Holder...PDA has received a great deal of input on the standards set forth [in October 2007]....Enclosed please find a new document titled 'Revised Standards and Procedure for the Approval of Proposed Labeling of Fluid Milk' dated January 17, 2008....Please review this document carefully and govern yourself accordingly....

From the revised standard:

"7. Label Representations.

(A) No labeling may be false or misleading....

    i. In no instance shall any label state or imply that milk from cows not treated with recombinant bovine somatotropin (rBST, rbST, RBST, or rbst) differs in composition from milk products made with milk from treated cows....

    ii. No labeling may contain references such as 'No Hormones, Hormone Free,....'

    iii. References such as "No rBST," "rBST Free," "Free of rBST," "No added rBST" may be considered misleading labeling based upon the entirety of the particular label under review.

By way of guidance, a label containing such references may be approved if such references are part of language defined in paragraph 7(B) as a "Claim," and is accompanied as set forth in paragraph 7(B) by a "Disclaimer." An example of such a Claim and Disclaimer would be "No rBST was used on cows producing this milk. No significant difference has been shown between milk derived from rBST-treated and non-rBST-treated cows." In such cases, the reference "No rBST," or the other references listed above, may be accentuated by different type style or size but not more than twice the size of the other Milk Labeling Standards 2.0.1.17.08 language in the Claim and Disclaimer....

(B) Permitted Claims. The following claims are permitted:

  (i) RBST (referenced to FDA February 10, 1994 Guidance on the Voluntary Labeling of Milk....)

   1. 'From cows not treated with rBST. No significant difference has been found between milk derived from rBST-treated and non-rBST treated cows' or a substantial equivalent. Hereinafter, the first sentence shall be referred to as the 'Claim' and the second sentence shall be referred to as the 'Disclaimer....'"

...

(Standards 2.0.1.17.08. http://www.portal.state.pa.us/portal/server.pt/gateway/PTARGS_0_2_24476_10297_0_43/AgWebsite/Files/Publications/milk_labeling_standards_new.pdf)

## Advocates Opposing the Ban Reflect on the Outcome

### "A Day for Celebration and Humility"

By Brian Snyder, Pennsylvania Association for Sustainable Agriculture. E-mail, January 1, 2008

This is truly a cause for celebration for all of us, especially those who responded to our alerts by sending letters and emails or making phone calls to Governor Rendell's office and the Pennsylvania Department of Agriculture....This is also a day for reflection and humility. There were many farmers on both sides of this issue right from the start, and the damage done to the agricultural community in Pennsylvania will take some time to heal....Yesterday's announcement preserved the right of farmers to communicate with eaters about the way food is being produced in a straightforward way. If you think about it, this is just about as fundamental as it gets.

## News Media Reports Ongoing Advocacy Supporting the Ban

### "Fighting on a Battlefield the Size of a Postage Stamp"
By Andrew Martin, The Feed, NYTimes.com, March 9, 2009. http://www.nytimes.com/2008/03/09/business/09feed.html

A new advocacy group closely tied to Monsanto has started a counteroffensive to stop the proliferation of milk that comes from cows that aren't treated with synthetic bovine growth hormone. The group, called American Farmers for the Advancement and Conservation of Technology, or Afact, says it is a grass-roots organization that came together to defend members' right to use recombinant bovine somatotropin, also known as rBST or rBGH....

## National News Media Reports Continuing Debate

### "'Hormone-free' milk spurs labeling debate"
*Christian Science Monitor,* April 21, 2008. http://www.csmonitor.com/Environment/2008/0421/p13s01-sten.html

Ohio, Missouri, Kansas, Indiana, and Michigan all have pending legislation or rule changes that would limit labeling claims about hormones....Some say Monsanto is behind attempts to remove mentions of hormones. "Clearly what's going on is Monsanto is trying to get states to thwart the market from working," says Michael Hansen, senior scientist for Consumers Union....But Monsanto contends that milk from cows treated with [its rBST product called] Posilac is safe....Monsanto has unsuccessfully petitioned the Federal Trade Commission for a rule change about what it says is deceptive labeling. Other legal action taken by the company and lobbying by farm bureaus to block such labeling has largely failed. Legal precedent appears to uphold the free-speech interest of dairies and the consumer's right to know...As other new agricultural technology reaches the market, labeling debates appear likely to increase, industry analysts say. For example, milk made from cloned animals and their offspring, approved January 15, 2008 by the FDA, has already prompted one labeling bill in California…"This [milk labeling] issue will not go away," says the Consumer Union's Mr. Hansen.

<hr>

**WHAT THIS CASE SHOWS.** Common features of policy making are illustrated here. For example, this case shows typical complexity in defining the problem. At least five policy problems with associated issues are conceivable in this case: (1) agricultural biotechnology with issues of impacts on people, animals, and ecosystems; (2) food safety with issues of consumer protection; (3) labeling with issues of free speech; (4) trade with issues of marketing and advertising; (5) ethics with issues of conflicting values. These conceptions of the problem are not mutually exclusive. That's typical, too. Problems usually are blends.

Solutions are selective. Policy analysis considers the options. In this case, basic options were considered. The state could accept the status quo without further action, or it could intervene, perhaps with limitations. To accept the status quo, Pennsylvania could follow federal FDA guidelines that allow rBST use in milk production and do not call for labeling. Instead, the state chose to regulate labeling, first to ban a specific practice, then later to allow it with limitations.

In the governmental framework, all three branches, the legislature, executive and administration, and judiciary make public policy. This case illustrates administrative policy making that involves federal and state government. The federal agency acted to the limit of its authority to monitor food safety, where the state agency went on to act within its authority to monitor product labeling.

Debate about the use of scientific evidence in policy making emerged in this case. On the subject of rBST use, U.S., Canadian, and European Union policies differ, with the United States permitting the use and the other governments not permitting it. The variation is attributable partly to different interpretations of evidence and partly to international differences in regulatory agencies' power.

Communication technology's impact on public process is evident in this case. Far exceeding print media's impact on opinion in rural communities, the Internet's capacity to rapidly distribute information by e-mail, online news, blogs, chat, and other media altered and accelerated Pennsylvania's process. Elsewhere, in other states, the network of information helped to organize interest groups across boundaries as more state governments took up the problem. Continuing access to online news archives kept the unofficial public record open and the issues alive as the problem moved beyond Pennsylvania.

Policy making is not always as topical or as visible as in the milk-labeling case. Important policy work goes quietly on every day in governance. Budgeting is a good example. Communications move a budget cycle along. To illustrate, an actual state budget development is described next, shown from the viewpoint of the communications director for the state senate's budget committee chairman.

## Case 2: State Budgeting

The annual state budgeting process occurs over six months with preset deadlines or milestones. In January, the governor proposes a budget for the coming year that represents the administration's priorities and politics. The legislative committees respond in March (for the house) and in May (for the senate) with recommendations based on their priorities and politics. Effectively, three budget proposals—the governor's, the house's, and the senate's—must culminate in a single adopted budget by July 1, the mandated start of the state's new fiscal year.

In early January, a state governor holds a press conference to announce the release of his proposed budget for the coming year. Immediately after the governor's press conference, the chairs of the state's house of representatives and senate budget committees comment publicly on the governor's proposed budget in other press conferences, newspaper interviews, and radio and television talk show appearances. The communications director for the senate budget chair tracks public response to the governor's budget and to the senate chair's comments on it.

At the same time, work begins on the senate and house budget recommendations. In the senate, the current chair of the ways and means committee brings his staff (an administrative assistant and the communications director) to a meeting with staff for the permanent committee. Present are the ways and means chief of staff, chief legal counsel, and chief budget analyst. The chair has authority, as a member of the majority political party, to set the senate's current budget policy. The permanent committee staff has responsibility for developing, with the help of the chair's staff, the senate's recommendations for budgeting according to current priorities.

In the first meeting in January, the chair and the combined staffs review budget history (what's carried over from last year and what's new this year), the state of the economy (current and projected conditions), and the politics of individual budget items (item is nice to have but can be sacrificed if necessary, item is nonnegotiable, we expect a fight on the item, or we go to the mat with the item). They compile a rough list of potential priorities for the coming year's budget. Because he will draft text for the senate recommendations, the communications director starts taking notes.

After the first meeting, the committee staff fans out in January and February to consult with federal and state fiscal experts, as well as with experts on specific issues in state agencies, government watchdog groups, and advocacy groups. They get more projections for the economy, and they seek external corroboration for their rough list of budget priorities. The communications director goes along to all these consultations.

Next, the committee staff solicits budget requests internally from senate members, state departments, and state agencies. Staffers meet with the members, departments, and agencies about their requests. They begin an initial breakdown of line items to include in the senate recommendations. The communications director stays in touch with the staff. In parallel, he maintains daily or weekly contact with editors and reporters of major news media. He develops relationships and educates the press. They, in turn, keep him up to date on budget-relevant news. He maintains good contact both internally and externally because he has dual responsibilities to anticipate debate about the senate's recommendations and to present them in a way that will promote their acceptance by government officials and the public.

A second working meeting is held. The chair and combined staffs intensely debate priorities and preliminarily decide on key priorities. Later in March, when the house budget proposal is released, the combined staffs analyze it, compare it with the governor's proposal, and compare it with their own developing proposal. The communications director participates in the meetings and continues to track press and public responses to the governor's proposal and to the house recommendations. Most important, he translates the key priorities (decided at the second working meeting) into key messages, simple statements that identify a key issue, and the senate's proposed way of using tax dollars to address the issue. He gets the chair's and committee senior staff's commitment to emphasize the key messages at every communication opportunity. Whenever they speak or write, they agree that the key messages will be appropriately included.

Throughout March and April, the senate budget committee staff finalizes its recommendations and interacts with the governor's and house committee's staffs. The communications director's attention increasingly turns to his primary responsibility of drafting the document that will both present senate recommendations and publicize them; he must also prepare for debate in the legislature and for negotiation with the governor's office during the budget approval process.

In March, he writes preliminary drafts of the chairman's introduction and the executive summary for the document. (He knows that when the lengthy and detailed document is released, many people, including the press, will read only the chair's introduction and the executive summary.) He emphasizes the key messages in both. He writes (or edits senior staff's) descriptions of major budget categories (health care, education, housing, and so forth). From his notes taken in budget working meetings, he develops arguments to support proposed dollar figures for existing line items and new initiatives in each category.

Also in March, he plans a comprehensive internal and external presentation strategy to be carried out in June. Along with internal distribution to the governor, the legislature, and government departments and agencies, the senate's recommendations will be publicized through an external news media and public events campaign conducted before, during, and after formal release of the recommendations document.

In April and early May, he revises the document based on committee staffers' review of his preliminary drafts and edits of their drafts. He coordinates with news media and advocacy groups regarding a public relations campaign to accompany release of the senate recommendations. By mid-May, the finished 600-page document presenting the recommendations is delivered to the printer. He fields inquiries by the press and the public about the soon-to-be-released recommendations, and he focuses on writing, editing, and revising press releases; other public announcements; and the chairman's comments for the senate budget release press conference.

In late May, the senate recommendations are released, distributed, and announced. Simultaneously, the planned public relations campaign is conducted. Throughout June, while the senate and house debate the budget and the governor responds to their debates, events all around the state (preplanned jointly by the communications director and advocacy groups) direct public attention to senate priorities and funding proposals during "health care week" or "education week" or "citizenship assistance week." Meanwhile, back in the senate, the communications director puts out daily press releases, follows up phone contacts by the press or the public, and prepares comments for the chair's use in responding to unexpected developments, politically significant news, or budget controversies.

●━● **WHAT THIS CASE SHOWS.** The problem here is the need to finance state government operations and public services in the coming year. The problem-solving process is the annual budgeting cycle. The major actors are three elected officials (the governor and the chairs of the state senate and house of representatives budget committees). Five appointed professional staffs (the governor's, the two chairs', and the two committees') advise and assist the elected officials. Other players are experts inside and outside state government with knowledge on specific topics, policy analysts who will advise authorities on ways to approach the problem, and advocates representing special civic, commercial, or political interests in the solution. The resulting policy is a set of priorities and related recommendations for spending.

In this case, you might be able to see components of policymaking functioning in a flow of actions to conduct a process. In budgeting, basic institutional actions are to define priorities in relation to current conditions and goals; to review previous goals; to take reasoned positions on needs, argue for them, and negotiate with others who reason differently; to propose specific objectives and spending levels; to deliberate alternative proposals and decide; and to inform and invite public participation. The flow of activity in this particular process is typical of institutional policy making.

Typical integration of communication and action is shown here, too. Communication products formalize conceptions and enable further action. For example, what most people call "the budget" is not the policy itself but, rather, an intentionally persuasive document (composed by the communications director, in this instance) that argues for objectives based on the priorities and that proposes funding allocations to accomplish them. It is the last of many documents that move the process along. At earlier stages, working discussions are materialized in draft documents. Circulation of the drafts for comment, editing, and revision facilitates negotiation about priorities. The final budget document serves both general public discourse (persuasive expression of priorities and objectives) and institutional discourse (dollar amounts) about governmental spending in the coming year.

Practical communications in this case deserve comment, too. From a communicator's viewpoint, budgeting, while orderly as a policy cycle, is quite messy as a real process. The case illustrates the typical density of information, number of writing demands, need to balance competing interests, need to coordinate actors, even the juggling of schedules that characterize a policy process and create the working conditions for communicators.

Detailed exemplification such as the milk labeling and budgeting cases gives you a material, real-time view of the policy process. Visualization gives you an abstract view. Figure 1.1 visualizes the phases of policy making as a circular progression of discrete and different actions.

In Figure 1.1, generating public interest and selecting a problem flow into designing a policy solution and deciding on a course of action to carry out its intent. Decision then progresses to implementation and administration labeled in the graphic as output, impact, and outcome. Implementation continues through evaluation, which leads

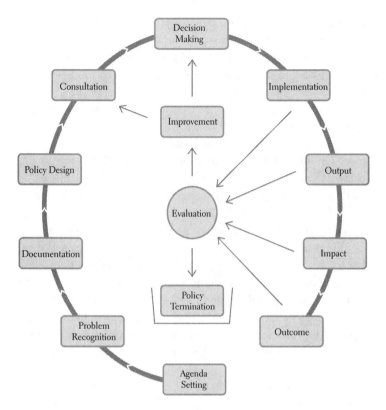

**Figure 1.1** The public policy cycle (By permission of Jan Ehrler, inffab, Switzerland).

to decision either to improve and continue the policy or to terminate it. Communication necessary to each phase is not shown. Instead, a separate category, documentation, appears early in this abstract view as an indicator of written (and spoken) necessary communication.

Like the list of policy actions in the preface to this book, Figure 1.1 simplifies reality. This cyclic view portrays policy making as progressing (lines and arrows) predictably through distinct phases (boxes). While it's too linear, a cyclic view nonetheless is helpful, if only because it encourages optimism. When you are immersed in grinding details or frustrating politics of policy work and it feels as if you are getting nowhere, it's refreshing to remember that you are engaging a process, however messy, with short-term objectives and long-term goals.

## Summary and Preview

Public policy making has three basic components: the problem, the policy, and the process. A problem is a perceived wrong in society or its environment. A policy is a standing decision by government. The process is problem solving in pluralistic politics and a governmental framework.

Next, chapter 2 explains how communication functions in the process and offers a disciplined approach to policy writing and speaking.

## Reference

Coplin, W. D., and M. K. O'Leary. 1998. *Public policy skills.* 3rd ed. Washington, DC: Policy Studies Associates.

## Further Reading

Coplin, W. D. 2007. *The Maxwell manual for good citizenship: Public policy skills in action.* Croton-on-Hudson, NY: Policy Studies Association.

Baumgartner, F. R., and B. D. Jones. 1993. *Agendas and instability in American politics.* Chicago: University of Chicago Press.

Baumgartner, F. R., and B.D. Jones. 2002. *Policy dynamics.* Chicago: The University of Chicago Press.

Kingdon, J. W. 2003. *Agendas, alternatives, and public policies.* 2nd ed. New York: Longman.

Sabatier, P., ed. 1999. *Theories of the policy process.* Boulder, CO: Westview Press.

Stone, D. 2002. *Policy paradox: The art of political decision making.* Rev. ed. New York: W.W. Norton.

CHAPTER $2$

# Communicating in the Process

## Key Concepts

- communicating in the context
- communicating in the process
- planning and producing useful written communications

Policy communication requires both know-how and skills. To develop know-how or conceptual understanding, this chapter describes communication to do policy work from four viewpoints. Each brings out a different dimension or highlights different variables in the activity. A cultural view characterizes the context. An experience view shows what happens in the doing. A process view traces the transformation of thought into written product. A methodology constructs a framework for producing the needed documents (or talks). Subsequent chapters invite you to apply these viewpoints strategically to practical communications.

## Viewpoint 1: Cultural Context—Actors, Roles, and Communication Practices

Who generates public policy information? Actors in the policy making process do. Actors are participants. Actors create and use information in accordance with their roles in the process. As the term is used here, a role is a function or job with specific responsibility in the process.

Interests motivate actors and influence their role performance. Interests are stakes or concerns, which might be organized (collectively held, ready for action) or unorganized (individually held, latent). For example, a trade association or an advocacy group has organized interest, whereas a dispersed, affected population has unorganized interest. Typically, organized interests acting as groups are most influential. However, individuals acting alone can be influential, too.

For all actors, roles and interests might relate in complex ways, and lines between them can be unclear. Some ambiguity is normal, as when an elected officeholder represents constituency interests in seeking a particular committee assignment or in proposing legislation. But other ambiguity might be unethical, as when an officeholder communicates false or misleading information. Ethics guidelines and enforcement procedures, internal and external to government, protect the policy making process. Even better protection comes from consciously ethical actors who aim to do no harm.

Typical actors in public policy processes include the following:

- providers of goods, services, or activities related to the problem
- consumers of goods or services in the problem area (if organized)
- experts with specialized knowledge of the problem
- advocates and lobbyists representing specific interests in the problem
- advocates representing the public interest in the problem
- officials with authority to solve the problem

For example, in making policy for highway safety, the following actors would be involved:

- automotive and insurance industries as providers of goods, services, or activities
- organizations of automobile drivers as consumers
- specialists in automobile design or analysts of the economics of transportation as experts
- lobbyists for law-enforcement associations as representatives of specific interests

- advocates for accident victims as representatives of the public interest

- members of Congress, cabinet secretaries, or state governors as official authorities

Whether they write or speak themselves or they authorize others to do it for them, policy actors generate information in relation to their role. Credibility, or the perceived reliability of information, is judged partly on the information source's role in the process. In the auto safety example, automotive industries credibly generate technical information on safety features of vehicles. Similarly, insurance industries credibly generate information on the economic consequences of accidents. Consumer groups credibly provide accounts of experience in using automotive products and credibly identify problematic conditions. Specialists in automobile design or materials credibly report results of research on ways to make cars safer. Expert policy analysts might credibly offer advice on policy options, such as regulation of manufacturers versus education of consumers. Advocates and lobbyists might credibly provide germane information about interested or affected groups, propose policy, and argue for or against policy based on group interests. Elected and appointed officials credibly generate the policy instruments, for instance, to reallocate funds, create a new program, or provide more oversight for existing programs.

Practical communications utilize forms conventionally expected to achieve a role's functions and particular purposes. Recall the typical actor roles in a policy process presented earlier in this chapter. For some of them, note the following examples of role-related practical communications. Elected and appointed legislative officials use bills and resolutions. Administrative officials use executive orders, statutes, legal codifications, standards and rules of enforcement, manuals, and press releases. (You can learn more about legislative and administrative communications in chapter 5 on government records research, where you are referred to respected sources, such as the Library of Congress's database *Thomas*, which includes glossaries of government document types.) Advocates use position papers, research reports, action alerts, press releases, letters to legislators, and witness testimony.

To suggest the range of practical policy communications, a listing that sorts actors by role and associated communication practices is provided next.

### Professionals Inside Government

Within government, career or consulting professionals generate most of the working information of a policy process. They communicate in roles as, for example, legislative aides to members of a legislature, experts on the staffs of legislative committees, legal counsels to legislative committees and agencies, executive agency administrators, policy analysts, and technical specialists attached to many offices. To carry out their responsibilities, they might use any of the following document types:

- one-pagers (summaries of fact or perspective, limited to one page)
- memos (more developed summaries of varying length)
- white papers (extensive reportage or analysis including evidence)
- legislative concept proposals (outlines of model or idea or strategy for policy, without details)
- legislative histories (reports of government action or inaction, based on government records)
- committee reports (synthesis of committee decision and history of action on a topic)
- speeches (to be delivered by elected or appointed officials)
- testimonies (to be delivered by executives or professionals)

For some inside professionals, communication is the entire job. The communications director in the state budgeting case (chapter 1) is an example. A communications director is a generalist who:

- writes and produces internal documents of many kinds
- writes external public announcements of many kinds
- produces kits of information for news media to use

Other professional communicators in government are specialists. They include:

- speechwriters who draft talks for officials to deliver
- legislation writers who draft bills for deliberation and formulate laws for codification
- debate reporters who produce stenographic transcripts and the published records of deliberation and debate
- webmasters who maintain government websites

### Professionals Outside Government

Significant amounts of information used in policy making come from outside government. Experts of many kinds in universities, industries, policy institutes, nonprofit organizations, and businesses write or contribute to white papers, reports of many kinds, and testimonies. Because they are not constrained as government employees are from engaging in public debate, they may write opinion in print or online publications. The expert's blog in the milk-labeling case in chapter 1 exemplifies this practice. In addition, professionals and managers in publicly regulated industries and businesses might provide needed information.

For some outside professionals, communication for public policy purposes is the main focus of their job. Lobbyists are an example. They are experts in a subject and are employed by organizations to ensure that policy makers have information about the subject that is germane to the interests of the employing organizations and to ensure that policy makers are exposed to the full range of arguments on a given issue. Lobbyists might brief legislators and their staffs, or they might draft legislation for consideration. Policy analysts are a different example. They may be either inside or outside government. They are experts in using quantitative and qualitative methods to examine problems and options for solving problems. Analysts might advise policy makers on the choice of policy instruments or provide research results to aid the formulation of policy.

### Active Citizens

Ordinary people in daily life inform and influence public policy making when they:

- write or e-mail officials
- provide formal written remarks on their experience relevant to a problem or a policy in response to a call for comment

- testify about effects of a problem or a policy on their life or their livelihood
- conduct letter-writing campaigns, create e-mail lists, and use phone trees
- form a coalition to cooperate in solving a problem
- create a mechanism, such as a lawsuit or a boycott, to force response by institutional authorities
- lobby as a representative of civic organizations, trade associations, professional associations, communities of interest, or constituencies

The milk-labeling case in chapter 1 illustrates citizen participation in several of these ways.

In the culture of public policy work, communication is not sufficient, but it is necessary. What does communication do? These are its key functions:

1. Communication produces useful information. Useful information in a public-policy process has four major characteristics: it helps to solve problems, it serves action, it has consequences, and it is publicly accessible.

(i) Helps to solve problems: Every phase of a policy process—to frame a problem, to analyze issues, to argue approaches, to decide on solutions—demands information. Only relevant information helps, however. In deciding whether to provide information, always ask and answer these questions: To whom is this relevant? How will it help to solve the problem?

(ii) Serves action: In policy work, information makes things happen. In deciding whether and how to inform in a policy process, always ask and answer this question: What do I want this information to do?

(iii) Has consequences: A problem and its solution affect other problems and solutions in many contexts. Consequently, information's effects can be wide-ranging. In deciding whether and how to inform in a policy process, always ask and answer these questions: What is likely to happen as a result of this information? What impacts might this information have?

(iv) Is publicly accessible: Policy makers are answerable to the people who give them authority. Therefore, information used in public processes must be publicly available. Officially, it is recorded and preserved by government as an authoritative public record. Unofficially, news media of all kinds and people in everyday social interactions distribute information as well. In deciding whether and how to inform a policy process, always ask and answer this question: How will this information be made public?

2. Communication makes information intelligible. Intelligible here means understandable and applicable in context. Context means, narrowly, a particular policy cycle, or, broadly, government and its political environment. Intelligibility occurs when expectations are activated and met. In order for meaningful communication to occur, information presenters and recipients must have similar expectations.

What expectations? The most basic is interaction, or informational give and take between people. Presenters expect to give information. Audiences expect to receive information. That reciprocity is fundamental to human communication for any purpose.

Other expectations influence communication's effectiveness. Genre or communication type is powerfully influential. Some say that effective communication begins with making the right genre choice. That is the selection of an appropriate communication type (or skillful use of a prescribed type) fitted to the presenter's purpose, the recipient's purpose and the relevant policy process.

Other powerful influences on effectiveness are utility and credibility. In public policy work, communication must be useful. What matters most is not how much you, the writer or speaker, know. Rather, what matters most is how much your readers or listeners know after taking in what you say, and whether they trust your information.

Finally, policy communication is expected to be efficient. Information products must be coherent, concise, and to-the-point. Efficient communication is universally appreciated in policy making because working conditions demand it. Public policy work is information-overloaded. Especially in government and nonprofit organizations, time is scarce, schedules are nearly impossible, and attention is always fragmented. Rarely does anybody have patience for disorganized, wordy documents or talks without obvious and relevant purpose and authority.

In summary, the cultural view shows us that information functions best in a policy context when it meets expectations. That is, it succeeds when it can be comprehended quickly, recognized as relevant, trusted as accurate, traced to authoritative sources, and used with confidence.

## Viewpoint 2: Experience

How do expectations function in readers' and writers' minds? A second viewpoint on communication looks at it as intellectual experience. Here's a quick sketch of what recipients of a document or talk experience. The sketch represents the experience of reading a policy document for information. It could also represent listening to an oral summation of the document.

Recipients hunt and gather. As they attend to a communication, recipients make numerous quick, tacit decisions about the information and its presenter. These decisions shape what the recipients think the communication is about, for whom it's intended, who is presenting it, what motivates it, what its point is, and, most importantly, whether it matters. In other words, recipients derive from an actual communication's features a perceived version of it. This perception is the basis of the recipient's understanding of the communication's meaning. (The familiar saying "What this tells me is…" refers to this perception.) Recipients evaluate the perceived information and its source. For instance, as they hunt for structural cues in the text's layout, they judge the presenter to be competent in the subject and caring about the recipient's time and interest, or not. If they have a choice, they are choosing whether it's worth their time to continue reading (or listening). If they continue, they choose how they will proceed. Typical strategies are to skim all, or to dip in and out, or to read selectively, perhaps only the summary. Recipients' criteria for selection are functional, based on relevance.

Now, here is a sketch of the other side of the experience. This sketch puts you in the scene as the presenter.

There is a demand for information. You are responding to the demand alone or in a team of people. You (or you and the team) will present the information in a chosen type of communication. These are your possible working conditions: You might choose the way you will communicate, or you might use a prescribed form. You might have ready access to relevant information, or not. The recipients might be known to you, or not entirely. The recipients' uses for the information might be known to you, or not entirely. Your intentions or purpose for providing information or what you want your contribution to achieve might be clear to you, or not entirely. You are aware of (or your team agrees on) the perspective you will take, or not entirely. Similarly, you are sure of your position on the topic (and your team agrees with you), or not entirely. You have limited time. You (or you and the team) must decide how to plan and produce the information product in the time available. You know that your product might be the only means by which recipients will know what you think. You know that it must be designed to fit recipients' needs and circumstances, although you can't be sure what they will be for all recipients.

These sketches depict experience as it might occur in any setting of policy work. Whether the presenter is a policy student writing to an instructor or a policy professional writing to a legislator, the same intellectual activity is required. What goes into that activity?

A third viewpoint on policy communication brings out the relationship between a writer's thinking process and its manifestation in a written product.

## Viewpoint 3: Process into Product

Process means change. Change transforms one state of existence into a different state of existence. In this guide, the primary process is public policy making. In that process, problems are transformed into governmental or community solutions. Communication is an essential secondary process. Communication enacts another kind of change whereby thinking is transformed into symbolic representations in words (written or spoken) or images. The foundational elements of thinking for policy communication are knowledge, perspective, position, adaptation, and documentation. Table 2.1 defines these elements.

**Table 2.1** Elements of thinking for policy communication.

Knowledge = content

Perspective = frame, viewpoint

Position = commitment, message

Adaptation = application, accommodation to context

Documentation = form and presentation

Each of these elements has its internal dynamics and subtle inter-dependencies with other elements. However, those relationships are outside the scope of this overview. Here, the point is that these elements function to generate information for policy making.

How do these elements function? Table 2.2 shows the elements in action, as acts of thinking.

**Table 2.2** Thinking as action.

Know = have information and awareness

Perceive = interpret from a perspective

Posit = claim and support

Adapt = fit to purpose and context

Document = present in symbolic form

For communicative interaction, thinking must move from the presenter's mind onto the page or screen and into the recipient's mind. A presenter's thinking must manifest as observable features of an information product such as a written document. The product will serve as the interface between presenter's and recipient's minds. Table 2.3 associates elements of thinking with related product features.

**Table 2.3** Elements of thinking manifest in product features.

| Element | Product Feature |
| --- | --- |
| Knowledge | Content specific to the domain; indicators of familiarity with subject |
| Perspective | Characterization of content from a viewpoint |
| Position | Statement of message with disclosure of reasoning |
| Adaptation | Content made relevant to the context |
| Documentation | Genre, form, style appropriate to the demand |

To round out this process-into-product view of communication, consider the policy communicator's need for control. Hectic working conditions are likely, so a disciplined approach to writing or speaking is advised. Most important for control is a goal. Communicators who know what they want to achieve can better assess and resolve any constraints on achieving it. They can make wiser choices of strategy and tactics. Looking forward in this guide, in the "how to" section of each chapter you will find a suggested goal, objective, strategy, and tactics (sequenced tasks) for a particular communication type. Here, next, you will find a general approach to managing any policy communication.

In earlier times, public policy thinkers employed self-questioning to discover relevant information and valid arguments. It is a good methodology. So, this overview's fourth viewpoint on policy communication distills the required intellectual activity into a comprehensive set of questions. These questions constitute a methodical approach to writing (or speaking) that is fitted to the policymaking process and to the culture of policy communication. They translate the culture into questions you should routinely ask when you initiate a communication. At the end of the questions are two checklists of expected qualities that public policy documents or talks should exhibit. The checklists are intended for your use in assessing a policy communication you have produced.

Now, you should only read the outline and checklists for perspective and for familiarity. Later, when you have an actual need to communicate (for instance, in an academic course or a policy workplace), you should use both. Use the method to plan before you write. Use the checklists after you write. Make using them a habit.

If you have mainly classroom writing experience, you may be surprised by the method's questions. They represent policy workplace writing conditions. For quick orientation to workplace writing, see any basic professional communication textbook.

Ask and answer the method's questions to plan and produce a communication. They prompt you to consider all the usual aspects of a writing situation and to take note of significant particulars that might affect your work. Your answers to the questions are your guide to writing or planning the needed product.

Practice this questioning methodically (even if tediously at first) until it becomes routine. At first, jotting down your answers and keeping your notes nearby as you write will be helpful. Later, when you habitually use this method, you will comfortably adapt it to particular or unusual demands. A word of caution: even if you skip some questions, do not omit whole steps in the method. All the steps are needed to cover the basics. Omitting a step in the preparation wastes time when you are writing, or causes other trouble later.

If you are writing for someone else or if you are producing a document with many contributors (the state budgeting case in chapter

1 illustrates both), remember to consult with others as needed to answer the questions.

## Viewpoint 4:  General Method of Communicating in a Policy Process

**Step 1:** Prepare

First, ask questions about the policy process.

*Policy*

- To what policy action (underway or anticipated) does this communication relate?

- Does a policy already exist?

*Problem*

- What conditions are problematic?

- What problem do these conditions present?

- How do I define the problem?

- How do others define the problem?

*Actors*

- Who are the actors?

- What are their roles?

- What are their interests?

- Who else has a significant role or interest in the process?

*Politics*

- What are the major disagreements or conflicts?

- What are the major agreements or common interests?

- Which actors are most likely to influence the process or the outcome?

**Step 2:** Plan

Second, ask questions about the communication.

*Purpose*

- Why is this communication needed?

- What do I want to accomplish?

*Message*

- What is my message?

- How does my message differ from others on the topic?
- What argument will I make to support my message?
- How does my argument relate to others on the topic?

*Role*
- What is my role in this process?
- What is my interest in the outcome?

*Authority*
- Whose name will be on the document(s): Mine? Another's? An organization's?
- For whom does the communication speak?

*Reception*
- Who is (are) the named recipient(s)?
- Who will use the information?
- Will the document(s) be forwarded? Circulated? To whom? Represented? By whom?

*Response*
- What will recipients know after reading the document(s)? What will users of its information do?
- What is likely to happen as a consequence of this communication?

*Setting and Situation*
- What is the occasion? What is the time frame for communicating?
- Where, when, and how will this communication be presented?
- Where, when, and how will it be received? Used?

*Form and Medium*
- Is there a prescribed form, or do I choose?
- What is the appropriate medium for presentation and delivery? A written document? A telephone call? E-mail?

*Contents*
- What information will support the message?
- Where will a succinct statement of the message be placed?

- How should the contents be arranged to support the message?
- How will the document's design make information easy to find?

*Tone and Appearance*
- How do I want this communication to sound? What attitude do I want to convey?
- How do I want the document(s) to look? Is a style or layout prescribed, or do I choose how to present the contents?

*Document Management*
- Who will draft the document? Will there be collaborators?
- Who will review the draft? Who will revise it?

**Step 3:** Produce
Based on your preparation and planning, write the document. Do it in three separate passes: draft first, review second, and revise third. Do not mix the tasks. Separating those tasks allows you to manage your time and handle distractions while you write, and to communicate better in the end.

The tasks are outlined here. Use this outline to stay on track if you're working alone, or under pressure, or producing a short document. If you're collaborating or team-writing, or if you're creating a multidocument product (such as the budget described in chapter 1), adapt the task outline to your circumstances.

*Draft*
- Produce a complete working draft in accordance with your preparation and plan (your answers to the questions listed earlier).

*Review*
- Compare the draft to the plan and highlight any differences.
- Get additional review of the draft by others, if advisable.
- Refer to the checklists (shown next here) to assess the draft's effectiveness and quality and to highlight needs for revision.

*Revise*
- Make the changes called for by review.

## Two Checklists

---

**FEATURES OF EFFECTIVENESS.** A public policy communication is most likely to be useful if it addresses a specific audience about a specific problem, has a purpose related to a specific policy action, represents authority accurately, uses the appropriate form, and is designed for use.

☐ Addresses a specific audience about a specific problem: In policy work, time is scarce. Specifying a communication's audience or intended recipient(s) and the subject or problem saves thinking time for writer and reader (or speaker and listener). The information's relevance for the recipient should be made clear.

☐ Has a purpose related to a specific policy action: Policy cycles have several phases. Multiple actions and cycles are underway simultaneously. Timing matters. Agendas change. Stuff happens. Therefore, explicitly stating a communication's purpose and relevance to the recipient makes it more likely to get timely attention.

☐ Represents authority accurately: Policy communications do more than present information; they also represent a type of participation and power. For a policy communication to be taken seriously, to have influence, and to influence rightly, the communicator's role and status—a citizen with an opinion, an expert with an opinion, a spokesperson for a nongovernmental organization, a government official—must be accurately represented.

☐ Uses appropriate form: Settings of policy work have their own conventions for communicating. Use the document type, style, and tone of presentation that are expected for the purpose and that accommodate working conditions in the setting of its reception.

☐ Is designed for use: People's attention is easily distracted in settings of policy work. Dense, disorganized text will not be read or heard. For people to comprehend under conditions of time pressure and information overload, contents must be easy to find and to use. Written documents should chunk information, use subheadings, and organize details in bulleted lists or paragraphs or graphics. Spoken texts should cue listeners' attention with similar devices.

━━━━━

**◄━** MEASURES OF EXCELLENCE. No two communications are exactly alike, but every public policy communication should try to meet criteria for clarity, correctness, conciseness, and credibility.

- ☐ Clarity: the communication has a single message that intended recipients can find quickly, understand easily, recognize as relevant, and use.
- ☐ Correctness: the communication's information is accurate.
- ☐ Conciseness: the communication presents only necessary information in the fewest words possible, with aids for comprehension.
- ☐ Credibility: a communication's information can be trusted, traced, and used with confidence.

*Example*

For practice, apply this overview to an actual policy communication. Keep the four viewpoints in mind as you read a professional writing sample, a report by the Congressional Research Service. Note that because of space limitations, the full report is not shown. The complete summary is shown. At the summary's end, you will find access information for the full report.

# The Federal Food Safety System: A Primer

Renee Johnson
Specialist in Agriculture Policy
January 11, 2011
Congressional Research Service
7-5700
www.crs.gov
RS22600
CRS Report for Congress
Prepared for Members and Committees of Congress

## Summary

Numerous federal, state, and local agencies share responsibilities for regulating the safety of the U.S. food supply. Federal responsibility for food safety rests primarily with the Food and Drug Administration (FDA) and the U.S. Department of Agriculture (USDA). FDA, an agency of the Department of Health and Human Services, is responsible for ensuring the safety of all domestic and imported food products (except for most meats and poultry). FDA also has oversight of all seafood, fish, and shellfish products. USDA's Food Safety and Inspection Service (FSIS) regulates most meat and poultry and some egg products. State and local food safety authorities collaborate with federal agencies for inspection and other food safety functions, and they regulate retail food establishments.

The combined efforts of the food industry and government regulatory agencies often are credited with making the U.S. food supply among the safest in the world. However, critics view this system as lacking the organization, regulatory tools, and resources to adequately combat foodborne illness—as evidenced by a series of widely publicized food safety problems, including concerns about adulterated food and food ingredient imports, and illnesses linked to various types of fresh product, to peanut products, and to some meat and poultry products. Some critics also note that the organizational complexity of the U.S. food safety system as well as trends in U. S. food markets—for example, increasing imports as a share of U.S. food consumptions, increasing consumption of fresh often unprocessed foods—pose ongoing challenges to ensuring food safety.

The 111th Congress passed comprehensive food safety legislation in December 2010 (FDA Food Safety Modernization Act, P. L. 111–353). Although numerous agencies share responsibility for regulating food safety, this newly enacted legislation focused on foods regulated by FDA and amended FDA's existing structure and authorities, in particular the Federal Food, Drug, and Cosmetic Act (FFDCA, 21 U.S.C. §§ 301 *et seq.*). This newly enacted law is the largest expansion of FDA's food safety authorities since the 1930s; it does not directly address meat and poultry products under the jurisdiction of USDA. The 112th Congress will likely provide oversight and scrutiny over how the law is implemented, including FDA's coordination with other federal agencies such as USDA and the Department of Homeland Security (DHS).

In addition, some in Congress have long claimed that once FDA's food safety laws were amended and updated, it would be expected that Congress would next turn to amending laws and regulations governing USDA's meat and poultry products. Food safety incidents and concerns regarding USDA-regulated meat and poultry products are similarly well-documented. A series of bills were introduced and debated in the previous few Congresses. These bills may be re-introduced and debated in the 112th Congress.

(The full report can be found at opencrs.com/document/ RS22600/)

---

**⊷ WHAT THIS EXAMPLE SHOWS.** This report summary manifests the transformation of process-into-product. Knowledge, perspective, position, adaptation, and documentation are effectively represented.

The first paragraph identifies the subject, food supply safety policy. The policy actors, federal agencies and their state counterparts, are recognized. In broad strokes, the writer represents knowledge of the domain.

The second paragraph recognizes another actor, the private-sector food industry, before summarizing the consensus viewpoint that federal government and the industry have together achieved a safe U.S. food supply. Complication of this consensus view immediately follows. Cueing the reader with a "however," the writer introduces a disagreement that challenges the consensus. Critics point to a problem, foodborne illness, that has exposed gaps in protection of the food supply. The consensus and the critical viewpoints differ. The author's own perspective is neutral, as an informed observer rather than a partisan.

The third paragraph opens with a sentence introducing the primary actor who is also the report's intended recipient, the U.S. Congress. This legislative actor makes policy that agency actors will administer and industry actors will implement. With the primary actor ("who cares") in focus, attention shifts to that actor's concerns ("so what"). Again, in broad strokes, the author describes the previous 111th Congress's legislative solution to the problem of foodborne illness. Possible next steps by the 112th Congress are previewed. The preview is tailored to the policy cycle and timely for the legislators' purposes, agenda setting and problem recognition, at the start of a new session. This fitting of the report to recipients' particular purposes at a particular time shows adaptation.

Other features of the documentation adapt to recipients' fragmented attention and to their need for confidence in the report's accuracy:

- an advance summary tells readers what the report offers
- in that summary, four short sections (each a paragraph long) begin with a sentence telling the reader that paragraph's main point, followed by subsequent sentences that consistently fill in the point
- after first use, domain-specific vocabulary is immediately explained
- at the summary's end, citations enable readers to trace the writer's sources

Another way to recognize adaptation in this summary is to look at the story it tells. Policy communications, like other kinds, tell a story that has a beginning, middle, and end. Narrative structure has not been discussed yet in this overview, but it is worth discussing. You will encounter it again in chapter 4 on policy analysis and critical analysis of policy discourse. For now, look for the storyline in the CRS report sample.

The summary tells a story of agenda setting and problem recognition. As the story opens, government characters are poised to act further on a new law. The characters are legislators, bureaucrats, producers of goods, providers of services, consumers, and subject-matter experts. There are no heroes or villains, only ordinary characters performing their relative roles in a system of governance. A problem has emerged to reveal flaws in the system. Characters have previously devised a solution to the problem. Will that solution work as intended? Is it sufficient to solve the problem? To learn the answers, stay tuned.

This story helps to move the reader's attention along. It is compactly told in four sequenced paragraphs. The first paragraph, or prologue, sets the scene and introduces the lead actor. The second paragraph introduces supporting actors and the complication, a problem the readers care about and for which the solution is not obvious. The third paragraph examines the current situation. The fourth paragraph sets the stage for continued action.

## Summary and Preview

Multiple actors in varied roles communicate to do policy work. Distilled into a general method for practical writing and speaking, their working knowledge of the process and communication's role can instruct you. This method keeps you on track, enables you to produce under pressure, to behave ethically, and to be accountable. Use it to write a problem definition in chapter 3.

## Further Reading

Allison, L., and M. F. Williams. 2008. *Writing for the government.* The Allyn & Bacon Series in Technical Communication. New York: Pearson Longman.

Coplin, W. D. 2007. *The Maxwell manual for good citizenship: Public policy skills in action.* Croton-on-Hudson, NY: Policy Studies Association.

Svara, J. 2007. *The ethics primer for public administrators in government and nonprofit organizations.* Sudbury, MA: Jones and Bartlett Publishers.

Williams, Joseph M., and Gregory G. Colomb. 2012. *Style: The basics of clarity and grace,* 4th ed. Boston: Pearson Longman.

# CHAPTER 3

# Definition: Frame the Problem

## Key Concepts

- frame the problem as an advocate
- rhetorical awareness

This chapter focuses on defining a problem for the purpose of getting it onto the public policy agenda. Advocacy to gain policy makers' attention is emphasized here as a means of achieving that purpose.

How does public policy making begin? Typically, it starts with perception of a wrong. Somebody perceives a condition in society or the environment to be wrong. Perceptions differ, so conflict might be involved in defining the wrong as a problem that policy might solve. Or, cooperation might be involved.

Problems come to public attention and a public policy agenda in various ways. Sometimes the problem chooses you. Something happens, you are affected by it, and you seek public action to address the problem. The triggering event might be large-scale, as when the destructive hurricanes Katrina and Rita damaged American coastal cities and states in 2005. Large-scale need for assistance followed, as individuals, families, local governments, and other collectives sought compensation or other action from federal government. Because after-action reports and investigations showed flaws in governmental storm response, policy makers reviewed and subsequently reformed national emergency management guidance for all hazards, including weather hazards. As in this case, chance events such as major storms can open a "policy window" of opportunity for change (Kingdon

2003). In contrast, a motivating event might be small-scale, even personal and singular. Following a child's death owing to a drunk driver, a parent formed the national nonprofit organization Mothers Against Drunk Driving (MADD) to influence law-enforcement standards for drunk driving.

Sometimes you choose the problem. Choosers vary. Inside government, elected and appointed officials have authority to decide what is and is not a problem and which problems will receive attention. In the budgeting case (chapter 1), a governor and state legislative committees exemplify this kind of chooser. The food-labeling case (chapter 1) shows a state administrative agency head selecting a food product for regulation. A writing sample shows a federal administrative agency policy analyst choosing military healthcare benefits for policy reform (Example 1, this chapter). Outside government, a chooser might be an advocacy group or a coalition of groups that brings a problem to legislators' attention, as when a farmer coalition advocates for changes in food safety bills (Scenario 2, Examples 3 and 4, this chapter).

To influence policy making, the perception of a wrong is not enough. If public policy is to be a solution, the wrong must be defined as one that policy makers can address. For example, you might perceive that obesity is wrong because it harms individuals, but individual solutions cannot be legislated. However, if you define obesity as a public health problem, you can relate obesity to public health standards or to medical research in the causes of disease. Those are problems with broad societal significance that can be addressed by policy makers.

Problem definition is important. As the logical first move in a policy process, problem definition sets the topics and direction for debate. Definition also predicts solution. You point to a solution by the way you define the problem. Different definitions lead to different solutions. For example, even though health authorities define obesity as a health problem, the numbers of overweight and obese people especially in the United States continue to rise. Why, you wonder, are people fat despite health warnings? Your question redefines the problem, thereby revealing different potential solutions. By focusing on the experience of people in everyday life, you expose another set of conditions relevant to obesity, behavioral issues such as eating habits, physiological issues such as genetics, cultural issues such as food preferences, economic conditions such as food costs, and economic interests such as food-industry profits. You point to solutions involving consumers, educators, businesses, and industries rather than healthcare providers.

Problem definition takes differences of perception into account. To a large degree, problem definition is subjective. One constituency's problem is another's acceptable status quo. Narrow and exclusive problem definition freezes possibility and invites competing solutions. Broad and inclusive definition imagines change and invites solution by coalition. In practice, problem definition is also rhetorical. Practical rhetoric is interaction between people or between organizations. The problem definer's awareness of rhetoric or interaction (who am I? whom do I address? how do I define the problem? how do others define it?) is a sensing device, bringing assumptions and values to light and exposing potential conflict or cooperation.

No matter how messy a policy process becomes, your action is directed by your definition of the problem.

## How to Define a Policy Problem

*Goal*: ability to recognize problematic conditions, to frame the policy problem they present as you see it, to be aware of your perspective and your purpose
*Objective*: purposeful depiction of the problem
*Product*: a short (1 page) or longer (20 or more pages) document
*Scope*: individual or collective; local or broader in impact; well-known or unrecognized; widely discussed or little considered; past, present, or anticipated
*Strategy*: provide information necessary for your purpose

Expect to be flexible in the writing process. Problem definition is usually iterative. After completing a task, you might find that you must revise earlier work. Or, after defining a problem, you might find that you want to, or you must, redefine it because conditions have changed or you have gained more knowledge.

### Get a Problem onto the Public Agenda
You want to bring public attention to a problem of concern to you. It might be known to others, but only recently familiar to you. Or you

might be aware of an unnoticed aspect of a known problem. Or you might be aware of a not-yet recognized problem. In any case, you must understand problematic conditions well. Also, you must know who cares and why they care.

To develop your knowledge, follow an approach of observation and inquiry. Do the tasks listed here in sequence. Results of one task will help you perform the next one. Note: this task outline assumes that you are a novice in problem definition.

### Task #1: Describe the Problem and Identify the Interests

First, describe the problem and identify the interested parties. This involves recognizing problematic conditions, identifying the problem that those conditions create, and specifying individuals as well as collectives that have a stake in the problem or its solution. To increase your awareness of problematic conditions and to recognize interests in it, you can proceed in any of the following ways:

- Work from observation of experiences, practices, effects:
  - Note likes/dislikes about your (or others') daily routine.
  - List good/bad aspects of your current or past job(s) or a family member's or a friend's job(s).
  - Sit for an hour in the office of a service provider to observe people affected by the problem and to observe the practices of policy implementers.
  - Visit locales affected by the problem to observe impacts.

- Work from subjective constructions:
  - Listen to or read or write stories (actual or imagined) that refer to the problem.
  - Describe the problem from a viewpoint, then describe it again from a different viewpoint.

- Work from unfinished business:
  - Reexamine a neglected need.
  - Revive a former interest.
  - Return to an incomplete project.

- Work from anticipation:
  - Imagine the consequences if things continue as they are.

- Imagine the consequences if things are changed as you advocate.
- Work from ignorance:
  - Choose a matter that concerns others (but is unfamiliar to you) that you want to know more about.
- Work from knowledge:
  - Consider the concern technically, informed by your (or others') expertise.
- Work from values:
  - Consider the concern ethically or legally, informed by your (or others') ideals or commitments.

## Task #2: Specify the Issues

When a problem has been identified, it is not yet a policy matter until its issues for policy are specified. Issues refer to stakeholders' concerns, political disagreements, and value conflicts. To recognize such issues, you might:

- Think about impacts of the problem. Who or what is affected by it?
- Conceive the problem narrowly and then broadly. Is it individual and local or more widespread?
- Conceive it broadly and then narrowly. Is it widely distributed or concentrated?
- Think about attitudes. How do different stakeholders perceive the problem? What values (ideals, beliefs, assumptions) are expressed in their definitions?
- Think about authority. How do stakeholders want to address the problem? Do they see government action as a solution? Do they agree or disagree on government's role?

## Task #3: Offer Solutions (If You Are Proposing a Solution)

Solutions typically rely on policy instruments that government can use (Bardach 2011). These include actions such as spending more or spending less and starting or ending programs. If you already have a positive and feasible solution to suggest, do so. (Generally, problem descriptions with a proposed solution get more attention.)

If you don't have a proposal, or if you want to counter a proposal, or if you want to create alternatives, stimulate your thinking with any of these approaches:

- Review the problematic conditions with a fresh eye, looking for unnoticed solutions.
- Reconsider a tried-but-failed or a known-but-ignored solution to find new potential.
- Look at the problem from a different perspective (a different stakeholder's, for example).
- Assign it to a different governmental level or jurisdiction if government already addresses the problem.
- Consult with nonprofit groups and nongovernmental organizations that are concerned about the problem.
- Consider doing nothing (keep things as they are).

## Task #4: Write the Document—Problem Description

Before you write, use the Method (chapter 2) to make yourself aware of the rhetorical framework (audience, purpose, context, situation) for your communication. Write with that framework in mind.

Problem descriptions can be presented in varied genres or document types. If the genre is prescribed for you, use it in accordance with your rhetorical framework. If you are free to choose, use a genre that fits your audience, purpose, context, and situation. These are commonly chosen options:

- letter, memorandum, or brief describing problematic conditions, possibly identifying causes of the conditions, and stating the problem
- letter, memorandum, or position paper conveying informed opinion, possibly advocating an approach to the problem

Here, next, you can see examples of problem descriptions in memorandum, report, position statement, brief, and proposal form. For sample letters and other resources for problem description go to these respected sources:

- *CQ Weekly Report, CQ Researcher Online, CQ Researchers Database* available in print in subscribing libraries or online at http://library.cqpress.com
- Opinion sections of national newspapers such as the *New York Times* (http://www.nytimes.com), *Los Angeles Times* (http://www.latimes.com), *Chicago Sun-Times* (http://www.suntimes.com), or *Washington Post* (http://www.washpost.com)

Problem descriptions in any form are expected to answer the following questions:

- What are the problematic conditions? What problem do they cause?
- What are the issues for policy?
- What is your concern? What is your intended reader's concern?
- Who else is concerned (on all sides)?
- What are the key disagreements and agreements among those concerned?
- (optional) What plausible and realistic solution can you offer?

You must cite the sources to which your problem description refers. Use the citation style prescribed, or choose either the American Psychological Association (APA) style (described at http://www. apastyle.org/learn/faqs/index.aspx) or the Modern Language Association (MLA) style (described at http://www.mla.org/style). Both APA and MLA style guides tell you how to cite a range of source types including government documents. (For example, see Citing Government Information Sources Using MLA Style at http://knowledgecenter.unr.edu/help/manage/government_cite.aspx)

For further help with citing government sources, consult Garner and Smith's *The Complete Guide to Citing Government Information Resources: A Manual for Writers and Librarians* (rev. ed.).

After you write, check your document's quality against the checklists in chapter 2.

## Five Examples with Scenarios

Writing samples of problem definition by advocates are presented here. They were written by professionals acting in two policy processes, administrative reform of military health care and legislative reform of food supply safety. Scenarios precede the samples to provide context.

### Scenario 1

The Chief of Patient Information in the Surgeon General's Office, U.S. Reserve Armed Forces is the subject matter expert for clinical policy questions relating to health care eligibility and benefits, records administration, medical readiness, and associated Army policies and regulations. She conducts analyses to answer questions in her subject areas and she writes policy documents. Regarding health care eligibility, a problematic condition has caught her attention. While doing routine research to answer an eligibility question, she finds that reserve component soldiers are not eligible for many of the medical and dental benefits available to active component soldiers. Senior administrative officers have long been aware of this condition and they know that increased reserve deployments are worsening it. Senior administrators have previously defined the benefits gap as a policy problem and recommended legislative solutions involving changes to the Department of Defense's health program, without success.

In this context of inaction, the analyst has encountered a problem recognized by others but not, until recently, by her. With permission from her administrative superiors to revisit the problem, she makes the disparity in military health care benefits a focus of her graduate coursework in professional communication undertaken for continuing professional education. She utilizes an assignment to write a preliminary description of the problem (Example 1, here) to develop her knowledge of problematic conditions and to practice framing the problem for policy action.

*Example 1*

**MEMORANDUM**

*TO:* (Primary Audience—Still being determined)

*CC:* (Secondary Audience—Still being determined)

*FROM:* (Author)

*DATE:* (Date of publication)

*SUBJECT:* (Expansion of Healthcare Benefits
for Reserve Component Service Members)

**Overview of the Problem**

Three hundred thousand American citizens serve in the Reserve Armed Force (RAF), with the number increasing daily. Even though the Reserved Armed Force has devoted over 60 million man-days to the Global War on Terror, these Reserve Component (RC) Soldiers do not receive the same medical or dental benefits as their Active Component (AC) counterparts. Due to the different lifestyle of a RC Soldier compared to an AC Soldier and to the varying benefits, Reserve Armed Force units are struggling to meet medical readiness goals for worldwide deployments and operations.

## Problematic Conditions
**Current Operations Tempo:** The current operational tempo of the United States military requires both AC and RC units to deploy on regular and frequent rotations. The RAF was established with a 5:1 ratio of training to operational years of service. Currently, most RAF units are barely meeting a 2:1 ratio. The lack of dwell time between deployments requires Soldiers to maintain a much higher level of constant medical readiness.

**Lack of Outside Health Insurance / Financial Hardship:** While the majority of RAF Soldiers have civilian employment, the percentage with personal health insurance drops to less than 30% of the force. Even though enlistment contracts require Soldiers to maintain their medical readiness, many do not have personal insurance or the financial means to procure healthcare.

**Socioeconomic Status:** RAF Soldiers have an average annual income that is 50% less than the average Air National Guard service member. While the "Hometown Recruiting" program has reached small communities and rural areas previously untapped for military service, the majority of the resulting force consists of blue-collar or farm-dependent citizens with a lower than average socioeconomic status.

## The Problem
Too many RAF Soldiers are not medically ready for deployment or missions.

## Impact of the Problem
With the RAF quickly developing into an operational force, the United States depends on its service members to maintain a high state of medical readiness in preparation for worldwide deployments and missions. The lack of consistent healthcare benefits for RC Soldiers results in a national average of 23% Fully Medically Ready (FMR) Soldiers across the RAF. As a result, units are deploying to combat theaters with 10–15% fewer Soldiers than missions require. The resulting holes in coverage in security forces, logistics support, and medical providers in combat theaters are devastating the war fight and endangering the Soldiers that are able to fight, as they do not have the support they require.

## Potential Solutions

**Maintain Current System:** Maintaining the current policy of 90 days of healthcare benefits prior to arrival at mobilization station will alleviate a small portion of the medical and dental issues preventing Soldiers from deploying. The current system balances the cost of healthcare with the cost of "fixing" a Soldier. This system does not allow for the deployment of Soldiers with issues that are treatable, yet require more than 60–90 days for optimum medical care.

**Full Coverage for Alert:** Soldiers currently receive full healthcare benefits 90 days prior to their arrival at the mobilization station. While this allows for them to receive care for minor illnesses and annual appointments, it does not allow enough time for Soldiers to receive treatment for more serious, yet treatable illnesses, such as hypertension, gum disease, or dental issues requiring dentures. Extending full healthcare coverage to Soldiers immediately upon alert of the unit will allow for the treatment of 95% of all dental issues, and the majority of illnesses which do not otherwise disqualify for worldwide deployment.

**Full Coverage throughout Period of Service:** Extending full healthcare benefits to RC Soldiers (which would mirror the full Tricare coverage AC Soldiers receive) would allow Soldiers to maintain a healthier lifestyle through regular medical and dental appointments. The potential gains of preventive medicine would, over time, reduce the cost of reactionary medicine for RC Soldiers, resulting in higher readiness rates. Additionally, if healthcare costs were covered, Soldiers could be held accountable for their individual medical readiness under statutes of the Uniform Code of Military Justice.

## Next Steps

As the country continues to call upon our Reserve Component forces, it is critical that we establish a more thorough and dependable system of providing healthcare to RAF Soldiers. The discrepancy between benefits received by the AC and RC is monumental, despite the valiant service of both components on the battlefield. I challenge concerned citizens, leaders, and politicians to recognize the time and money being lost on professionally trained Soldiers who are unable to deploy due to preventable medical and dental issues. Disagreement with our country's position in the current war is unrelated to the benefits our Soldiers deserve for their service. Let us take care of the very men and women who are risking their lives for our country on the dangerous frontlines of the Global War on Terror by improving healthcare benefits regardless of duty status or military component.

---

•◦• **WHAT THIS EXAMPLE SHOWS.** Example 1 illustrates narrow problem definition focused on a single affected population. It provides expected information by answering required questions (Task 4, this chapter). It identifies problematic conditions, specifies a problem those conditions present, and proposes solution options. It makes no recommendations, except (perhaps inadvertently) in the draft memo's subject line. "Expansion of benefits" in the subject line is inconsistent with the "Potential Solutions" section of the document where alternatives are described but not chosen. As a genre, problem description might appropriately either include or omit recommendations. However, the communication's purpose must be clear. If this document's subject line more accurately said "Healthcare Benefits Disparity Requires Attention" it would avoid introducing a solution.

The weakness of Example 1 is omissions. It leaves basic questions unanswered (Task 4, this chapter). It does not identify other interested stakeholders or potential agreements and disagreements among interested parties. Perhaps stakeholders and interests are implied in the final paragraph subheaded "Next Steps." But that generalized paragraph does not pinpoint actors or their concerns. And, it does not specify steps to be taken. Finally, the document lacks credibility because it does not identify the writer or intended recipients. Explanation for this omission is that there is no policy action underway, so the purposes and audiences are not yet identifiable. Nonetheless, because it is incomplete and still a draft, the document is not ready for use in a policy process. However, it instructive for the writer by showing what remains to be done. It illustrates the demand for rethinking and rewriting as you iteratively define a problem. Omissions, even errors, can be instructive for writers.

To format this communication, the writer, a professional in government, appropriately chooses a written memorandum or memo (Method, Step 2, chapter 2). This is a common workplace genre intended for quick reading, easy understanding, and efficient refer-encing in meetings. (In colonial America, it was called a memorial, meaning information to be remembered.) Modern memos are orga-nized top-down, with an initial overview followed by topical sections, like the inverted pyramid of news articles. This organization and the memo's compact form fit the time, attention, and accountability demands of governmental workplaces.

Unlike a news article with a single headline, a memo has a header or stacked items identifying the communication's who (sender and addressed recipient), what (subject), why (purpose), and when (trans-mittal date). Additional intended recipients might be specified in a "cc" ("copied on this communication") item placed either in the header or at the document's end. The memo's subject is identified in the "re" ("regarding") line, which serves as the memo's title. Content is chunked into sections with subheadings (like mini-headlines) cue-ing readers to the particulars covered in each section.

In Example 1 capitalization ("S" in "Soldier," for instance) reflects prescribed style in the writer's workplace and is retained here.

---

### Scenario 2

Previously, you read a Congressional Research Service summary of the 2011 FDA Food Safety Modernization Act (chapter 2). That Act had a long prior legislative history. "Pure food" policy originat-ing in the 1930s generated a steady stream of federal legislative and administrative reforms intended to assure the safety of food that Americans consume. Over decades, congressional commit-tees, commissions, and taskforces worked with the endorsement of several presidents to create a body of laws, standards, and reg-ulations, as well as federal agencies responsible for administering them. After 2001 the U.S. "war on terror" added food security or protection against tampering and deliberate contamination to food safety policy.

These precedents focused on food manufacturing and distribu-tion. Food growing and handling on the farm were not addressed except for the initiation of a national system to identify and track meat animals. Opportunity to pull food growing and handling into the food safety net came between 2006 and 2011. At that time, random events, national elections, and political advocacy converged to enable reform. Illness outbreaks attributed to spinach (2006), eggs (2006), and peanuts (2009) renewed public perception of a food safety problem. National elections in 2008 shifted political power to a new majority in the legislature and administration. Citing illness outbreaks attributed to peanut processing, newly elected President Barack Obama announced the creation of a new interagency food safety working group. "We all eat peanut butter, including my daughters. We need to fix this," he said.

Interest advocacy geared up to influence legislative and administrative initiatives. Legislative committees in the House and Senate drafted new bills, held public hearings, requested reports from research and investigative services, and received advocates' advice on bill provisions. Administrative agencies received advocates' petitions for new rules and held hearings to collect public comment on them. Intense activity in 2009–2010 resulted in the landmark FDA Food Safety Modernization Act (FSMA) passed by the 111th Congress in December 2010 and signed by President Obama in January 2011. Administrative rule-making to set standards and create regulations for enforcement of the new law began in 2012.

Sample communications in that legislative process are shown next in this chapter. (Samples in the subsequent administrative process are shown in chapters 7 and 10.) Professionals in government or nonprofit organizations wrote these samples. Condensed versions are shown, with access information to the entire document provided.

*Example 2*

**FDA Has Begun to Take Action to Address Weaknesses in Food Safety Research, But Gaps Remain**
GAO-10-182R, May 24, 2010
Additional Materials:
Accessible Text
Contact:
Office of Public Affairs
(202) 512-4800
youngc1@gao.gov

Summary
The United States faces challenges to ensuring food safety. First, imported food makes up a substantial and growing portion of the U.S. food supply, with 60 percent of fresh fruits and vegetables and 80 percent of seafood coming from across our borders. In recent years, there has been an increase in reported outbreaks of foodborne illness associated with both domestic and imported produce. Second, we are increasingly eating foods that are consumed raw and that have often been associated with foodborne illness outbreaks, including leafy greens such as spinach. Finally, shifting demographics means that more of the U.S. population is, and increasingly will be, susceptible to foodborne illnesses. The risk of severe and life-threatening conditions caused by foodborne illnesses is higher for older adults, young children, pregnant women, and immune-compromised individuals.

In January 2007 GAO designated federal oversight of food safety as a high-risk area needing urgent attention and transformation because of the federal government's fragmented oversight of food safety. The Food and Drug Administration (FDA) is responsible for ensuring the safety of roughly 80 percent of the U.S. food supply—virtually all domestic and imported foods except for meat, poultry, and processed egg products—valued at a total of $466 billion annually, as of June 2008. In 2007 the FDA Science Board, an advisory board to the agency, reported that science at FDA suffers from serious deficiencies. In addition, our prior reviews of FDA's food safety programs have identified gaps in scientific information, limiting FDA's ability to oversee food labeling, fresh produce, and dietary supplements. Further, as part of our recent review on the effectiveness of the strategic planning and management efforts of FDA, 67 percent of FDA managers reported, in response to a GAO survey, that updated scientific technologies or other tools would greatly help them to contribute to FDA's goals and responsibilities; however, only 36 percent of managers reported that FDA was making great progress in keeping pace with scientific advances. In written comments responding to our survey, some managers stressed the need to increase and stabilize funding, recruit and retain top scientists, and make decisions on the basis of scientific evidence.

In this context, you asked us to examine ways in which FDA may use science to more effectively support its regulatory work and to inform the public about food content and safety. This report focuses primarily on FDA's (1) progress in addressing selected recommendations identified by the Science Board; (2) incorporation of scientific and risk analysis into its oversight of the accuracy of food labeling, fresh produce, and the safety of dietary supplements; and (3) a new computer screening tool that may improve its efforts to screen imports using a risk-based approach.

FDA has begun to address selected Science Board recommendations. For example, FDA reported in May 2008 that it created the Office of Chief Scientist and, in May 2009, it added more responsibilities to the office to signal a new emphasis on regulatory science. According to the Acting Chief Scientist, his office plans to identify major scientific cross-cutting opportunities across FDA and to collaborate with other government agencies. However, gaps in scientific information have hampered FDA's oversight of food labeling, fresh produce, and dietary supplements. In addition, FDA's new computer tool—PREDICT—is designed to improve its risk-based import screening efforts by analyzing food shipments using criteria that include a product's inherent food safety risk and the importer's violative history, among other things, to estimate each shipment's risk. FDA has developed a draft performance measurement plan for evaluating the effectiveness of this risk-based approach.

(The full report can be found at www.gao.gov/products/GAO-10–182R)

---

**⊷ WHAT THIS EXAMPLE SHOWS.** Example 2 exhibits many of the qualities in public policy communication that this guide supports (Checklists, chapter 2).

The Government Accountability Office (GAO) is a respected research, legal, and investigative agency of the Congress. Its reputation lends credibility to its reports. In addition, the document exhibits features of traceability and accountability that encourage readers to presume that the report's information is reliable. By stating (in a letter of transmittal not shown here) explicitly for whom the report speaks (GAO) and to whom it is addressed (a committee chairman) and by referring (in the full report) to review of this and prior reports by the agency concerned (FDA), this report is accountable.

The summary's organization anticipates the report's reception and use in hectic policy workplaces. It is compact. Content is coherent, with transitional markers such as "first...second...finally." Key information is easy to find, an especially important feature if the content will be condensed for oral briefings or discussed in public hearings. Within paragraphs, the information is ordered top-down or in general-to-particular logical order. Opening sentences summarize; following sentences elaborate. The summary's readers can rely on obvious transitions and repeated order of presentation to scan comprehendingly. Information hunter-gatherers can use these features to target their selections (Method, chapter 2).

The genre is a report. Government agencies such as GAO often require reports for specific communication purposes. GAO specifies formal written reports for communicating finished results of investigation requested by a Congress member. Institutions including government agencies sometimes also prescribe a house style of document design. GAO style for report summaries is illustrated here: three main sections (why the study was done, what was found, what is recommended). GAO style encourages use of subheadings such as Why GAO Did This Study, What GAO Found, and What GAO Recommends. This summary does not use subheadings. If it had, the report's readability would be even better.

The reader who accesses this report via the GAO website on the Internet will see the one-page summary that is reproduced here. Accompanying the summary, links go to the full 25-page report, to GAO contact information, and to an accessible version of the report. The latter version implements GAO's communication policy, which recognizes that many readers now seek governmental information via the Internet and that different readers have different Internet access capabilities (Appendix). The reader selecting "Accessible Text" will find an accompanying explanation of GAO's compliance with the Federal Web Managers Council's guidance "Provide Access for People with Disabilities (Section 508)." The guidance is publicly available at http://www.howto.gov/web-content. The explanation says "This text file was formatted by the U.S. Government Accountability Office (GAO) to be accessible to users with visual impairments, as part of a longer term project to improve GAO products' accessibility. Every attempt has been made to maintain the structural and data integrity of the original printed product....We welcome your feedback. Please e-mail your comments regarding the contents or accessibility features of this document to webmaster@ gao.gov."

---

**Scenario 2 continued**

As they developed a new bill in April 2009, staff members of the House of Representatives Commerce Committee met with advocates for sustainable agriculture. According to advocacy group mission statements, sustainable agriculture is farming that is ecologically sound, community supportive, and economically viable. Among topics discussed in the April meeting was advocates' objection to a "one size fits all" approach to safety regardless of farm size, scale, or type of operation. Committee staff asked for alternatives to consider. In response, an advocacy group representative wrote a position statement laying out a logic for making exceptions. The statement is presented next here.

---

*Example 3*

### A Message to Public Officials on Food Safety

By Brian Snyder, Executive Director Pennsylvania Association for Sustainable Agriculture (PASA) May 22, 2009

It seems everyone in elected office these days wants to do something about food safety....As a community of farmers, we must also come to terms with the fact that harmful pathogens occasionally present in food can originate on farms in various ways that at times defy easy explanation.

...

Now let us consider the desire folks in government have to devise a legislative solution for the problems of food safety....It is the acknowledged job of government to protect us to the extent possible from negligence and preventable forms of injury and/or death. But it is distinctly NOT the job of government to attempt to eliminate risk in life altogether, nor to impose expectations that may impinge unnecessarily on the free enterprise activities of the citizenry without a clearly understood benefit.

More than anything else right now, we need some plain talk on the real issues involving the safety of our food supply. With good science available on all sides, there is widespread disagreement about what matters most and why any of us should care.

We at PASA believe quite simply that the most important thing anyone can do to reduce risk in the food system is to make it as locally-based as possible. A safe food system is built on trust, and trust is built on actual human relationships. Such relationships are harder to maintain the larger and more diffuse the food system becomes.

Furthermore, we contend that the greatest risks to food safety occur when two systemic factors are combined: a) "food anonymity" and b) geographically broad distribution patterns. The most basic strategies for achieving a safe food supply, therefore, are not only to keep the distribution patterns as local and/or regional as possible, but also to put the farmers' faces back on the food. In an ideal scenario, both strategies would occur. Whatever else is said about specific practices on a farm or in a food processing facility, these two factors should be acknowledged as priorities and properly rewarded by the regulatory authorities right up front.

With this in mind, the following three-tiered structure seems both to be the current reality in food production and marketing systems, and a necessary framework for any successful effort to further regulate food safety and security:

1. Farm-direct—This includes farm stands, farmers' markets, community supported agriculture (CSA) programs (e.g. subscription farms) and other innovative strategies where the relationship between individual farmers and consumers is immediate and understood.

2. Identity-preserved—This involves distribution patterns on a regional scale where the farmer and consumer do not necessarily meet, but the identity of the farm is preserved on products all the way through the system, from field to fork.

3. Commodity stream—This represents sales where no direct relationship between farms and consumers exists. The farm identity is vague or lost altogether, sources are aggregated and distribution tends to be widespread, including food exported to other countries.

Taking them one at a time, we believe there should be minimal intervention by the government in regulating practices in the first tier, with respect to private transactions occurring between individual farms and consumers....Problems arising here can quite naturally be traced quickly and addressed effectively without associated threats to any broad segment of the population.

With the second tier, it is most important to understand that the government has a tremendous opportunity to take advantage of the good things currently happening out there. The goodwill and positive business practices of farmers, processors and retailers who are already participating in local and regional food system initiatives are ensuring a significant degree of traceability that should be supported in any way possible.

Let me say this as plainly as possible. The government has every right to set reasonable standards for food quality and safe production practices. Nonetheless, farmers with their names—and reputations—listed on every package of food should have options to work on a voluntary basis with independent, third-party entities of their choosing in meeting such standards. Such partnering entities might include certifiers of organic, sustainable or natural products, farm cooperatives, breed associations and other trade organizations with a direct interest in supporting best management practices on the farms they serve.

The third tier represents the vast majority of food product consumed in this country and almost all that is exported to others. The need here for clearly stated and enforced quality and safety standards is obvious and should be a central priority of any food-related legislative agenda in the immediate future....

The essential element here is not that there is some theoretical distinction between "good" and "bad" farmers....This is also not fundamentally an issue of "big farms" vs. "small farms," though it appears unavoidable that vocal contingents on both sides of that divide will try to make it so.

The most pressing concern right now is that, in the rush to do something productive on the most public aspects of safety and security in the food supply, our public officials might take action that will a) do too little, for fear of offending some of the powerful interests involved, or b) do too much and thereby inflict real damage onto one of the most promising trends in agriculture to come along in at least half a century.

...

But if we can really get this right, a visionary and "fresh" approach concerning food safety at local, state and federal levels of government might lead to an agricultural renaissance in this country that will do as much for the economic health of our rural communities as it will for the physical health of our people.

(The complete statement can be found at http://pasafarming.org/news/policy-statements.)

---

►━• **WHAT THIS EXAMPLE SHOWS.** This statement illustrates broad and inclusive problem definition. One indicator is its inclusive language. "We talk of policy problems in words. How words are used to represent things is a subject usually treated in the domains of rhetoric and literature, but symbolic representation is the essence of problem definition in politics" (Stone 2002, p. 137). Broad and inclusive definition combines topics and generalizes goals in order to expand the problem scope, to invite solution by coalition, and to envision comprehensive change. Expanded scope is shown by combinations such as "food safety and security" and "growers and processors." Potential for coalition is shown by "community of farmers" and "farmers of all stripes." Comprehensive change is represented by parallelism in the structure of sentences such as this one: "Do as much for the economic health of our rural communities as . . . for the physical health of our people." When characterizing actors in the process, the writer avoids stereotypes such as "agribusiness, large corporations, family farmers." He uses nonpolarizing, generic "farmers," instead. Similarly, the writer argues against thinking in simple dichotomies (e.g., "good" and "bad" farmers or "big farms" and "little farms").

Inclusiveness invites actors who disagree to work together. By framing the problem generally and by using an approachable, reasonable tone (Method, chapter 2), the statement invites consideration of alternatives.

A policy communicator's thinking is exhibited in the text (Viewpoint 3, chapter 2). The writer states the organization's perspective ("We at PASA believe . . .") explicitly before acknowledging other perspectives. The organization's position is that, because the food supply system is complex, solutions to the problem of food safety should be flexible (Method, chapter 2).

The statement answers all the questions a problem description is expected to answer (Task 4, this chapter.) It specifies causal conditions, the policy problem those conditions present as seen from the definer's perspective, and issues for policy consideration (e.g., risk standards, product traceability, compliance monitoring).

This advocate chose a written position statement to present the organization's advocacy. That genre is appropriate for addressing mixed audiences with both intended and potential readers (Viewpoint 3, chapter 2). Legislators and staff on specific congressional committees are intended readers, in this instance. Potential readers might be members of the writer's state-level organization, national partner organizations, and news media. For access, the advocacy statement appears on the "Press Room" page of the organization's website.

Organized as an informal opinion essay, the statement's style is nontechnical expression ("plain talk on the real issues") (Method, chapter 2). The statement purposefully blends essay and memo organization at a key point. To present informal analysis of the food supply system to support a logic for exemptions, the writer switches from essay to memo form. The "three-tiered structure" that is "a necessary framework...for reform" is enumerated in a list. Listing and numbering distinguish individual items; indenting surrounds the entire list with blank space. All these devices pull attention to the analysis (Method, chapter 2).

This advocacy statement does not make policy recommendations. For those, read the National Coalition of Sustainable Agriculture's position statement, next.

*Example 4*

### Food Safety on the Farm: Policy Brief
October 2009

For over twenty years, the National Sustainable Agriculture Coalition (NSAC) has advocated for federal agricultural policies that foster the long-term economic, social, and environmental sustainability of agriculture, natural resources, and rural and urban food systems and communities. NSAC's vision of agriculture is one where a safe, nutritious, and affordable food supply is produced by a legion of family farmers who make a decent living pursuing their trade, while protecting the environment, and contributing to the strength and stability of their communities. NSAC's work has resulted in federal programs that promote small and mid-sized family farms, increase new farming and ranching opportunities, invest in sustainable and organic research, reward conservation excellence, and expand local and regional food systems.

Over the last several years, the rise in major outbreaks of foodborne illnesses has called into question the sufficiency of the U.S. food safety system. Up until now, food safety regulatory oversight has focused mainly on processing, food handling, and manufacturing sectors—areas shown to be of highest risk for foodborne pathogen contamination. However, several food safety bills have been introduced into the 111th Congress that could directly or indirectly affect farms and ranches by expanding these authorities and making some on-farm safety standards mandatory. In addition, in the spring of 2009, the Obama Administration created an inter-agency Food Safety Working Group through which the Food and Drug Administration and U.S. Department of Agriculture are adopting new food safety standards and oversight, including on-farm measures.

While NSAC applauds Congress and the Administration for taking steps to decrease foodborne illnesses by strengthening federal food safety oversight and enforcement, in respect to farms it urges decision-makers to ensure that:

- Measures are risk-based, focus on risk reduction, and are justified by scientific research;

- FDA coordinates with other state and federal agencies and community-based organizations with food safety expertise or pre-existing standards or training programs for standard development and enforcement;

- Standards do not discriminate against, but rather encourage, diversified farming operations and conservation practices;

- Standards are appropriate to the scale of the enterprise;

- Fees of any kind, if they are imposed, are equitable to reflect different scales of production and ability to pay;

- Traceability rules for farmers should not require more than good, basic recordkeeping (one-up, one-down) of all sales;

- Marketing Agreements and Orders are not used to regulate food safety.

- NSAC members and food safety experts agree that the responsibility for ensuring that our food is safe is incumbent on all actors in the food supply chain: from farmers, packers, processors, and distributors, to the final consumer. It is our position, however, that proposals proffering one-size- fits-all solutions to food safety fail to acknowledge the diversity of agriculture and are inappropriate and counterproductive courses of action.

(The complete brief can be found at http://sustainableagriculture. net/wp-content/uploads/2008/08/NSAC-Food-Safety-Policy-Brief-October-2009.pdf.)

---

▬• WHAT THIS EXAMPLE SHOWS. This policy brief has a two-part structure, initial summary (presented in this chapter) followed by policy recommendations (presented in chapter 4).

In the summary shown here, a policy communicator's thinking is evident (Viewpoint 3, chapter 2). In the opening paragraph, the first sentence identifies the subject, long-term agriculture policy. The second sentence asserts the frame or perspective of the sustainable agriculture coalition. The third sentence justifies the frame by citing the coalition's authority based on knowledgeable experience and accomplishment in policy work.

The second paragraph initiates a problem description. Its first two sentences document causal conditions including triggering events, insufficient regulation, and inadequate policy responses. From the coalition's perspective, those conditions present a problem of governance. Solution to that problem is principled reform. A bulleted list of guiding principles adapted to the current problem, food supply safety, is offered. The list concludes with an assertion of the coalition's position that principled reform for the long term is better than short-term solutions. In two compact paragraphs, the summary efficiently represents all the elements of policy communication: knowledge, perspective, position, adaptation, and documentation.

---

**Scenario 2 continued**

---

As versions of food supply safety legislation progressed through the House over the summer of 2009, splits developed in the sustainable agriculture community's attitude toward reform. Advocates divided primarily around the logic for exemptions from new safety requirements. Some wanted to exempt farms, including those offering value-added products, based on the size of the operation, while others were more interested in protections related to the style and geographic breadth of marketing programs. During deliberations on the companion Senate bill in the fall of 2009 and 2010, an amendment proposed by Montana Democrat Senator (and organic farmer) Jon Tester and North Carolina Democrat Senator Kay Hagan included a solution that would exempt certain producers based on combined considerations of size and geography. In its final form, the Tester-Hagan amendment allowed for limited exemption of operations with less than $500,000 in annual gross revenue and all sales within the state of residence or 275 miles (if out of state), as long as the farm of origin is made clear on a placard or label. The sustainable agriculture community's debate changed in reaction to the amendment. Some advocates argued strongly for this solution but others continued to push for total exemption from federal government scrutiny for all small farms. Opponents argued that state and local public-health standards were sufficient food supply safety guards.

---

The Tester-Hagan amendment was accepted in the Senate Health, Education, and Labor Force Committee's bill. Later it was incorporated in the enrolled bill passed by both the House and the Senate. Also incorporated were related requirements for the FDA to assist small businesses in complying with the new law. These incorporations respond to advocates' concerns and demonstrate advocacy's influence on legislation. To illustrate that influence, sections of the final bill are shown next here.

*Example 5*
FDA Food Modernization Safety Act (H.R. 2751 ENR.)

**Title I: Improving Capacity to Prevent Food Safety Problems**
Sec. 102. Registration of Food Facilities
(b)Suspension of registration.
(2) Small entity compliance policy guide.—Not later than 180 days after the issuance of the regulations promulgated under section 415(b)(5) of the Federal Food, Drug, and Cosmetic Act (as added by this section), the Secretary shall issue a small entity compliance guide setting forth in plain language the requirements of such regulations to assist small entities in complying with registration requirements and other activities required under such section.
(c) Clarification of Intent.
(1) Retail food establishment.—The Secretary shall amend the definition of the term "retail food establishment" in section in 1.227(b)(11) of title 21, Code of Federal Regulations to clarify that, in determining the primary function of an establishment or a retail food establishment under such section, the sale of food products directly to consumers by such establishment and the sale of food directly to consumers by such retail food establishment include—
(A) the sale of such food products or food directly to consumers by such establishment at a roadside stand or farmers' market where such stand or market is located other than where the food was manufactured or processed;
(B) the sale and distribution of such food through a community supported agriculture program; and
(C) the sale and distribution of such food at any other such direct sales platform as determined by the Secretary.
(2) Definitions.—For purposes of paragraph (1)—
(A) the term "community supported agriculture program" has the same meaning given the term "community supported agriculture (CSA) program" in section 249.2 of title 7, Code of Federal Regulations or any successor legislation; and
(B) the term "consumer" does not include a business.

Sec. 103. Hazard Analysis and Risk-Based Preventive Controls.
(l). Modified Requirements for Qualified Facilities
(1) Qualified Facilities.—
(A) In general.—A facility is a qualified facility for purposes of this subsection if the facility meets the conditions under subparagraph (B) or (C).

(B) Very small business.—A facility is a qualified facility under this subparagraph—

...

(C) Limited annual monetary value of sales.—

(i) In general.—A facility is a qualified facility under this subparagraph if clause (ii) applies—

(ii) Average annual monetary value.—This clause applies if—

(I) In the 3-years preceding the applicable calendar year...

(II) the average monetary value of all food sold by such facility (or the collective average annual monetary value of such food sold by any subsidiary or affiliate...was less than $500,000 adjusted for inflation."

(The full bill can be found at H.R.2751 ENR. *FDA Food Safety Modernization Act.* Http://thomas.loc.gov/cgi-bin/query/z?c111:H.R.2751.)

----

**◆━ WHAT THIS EXAMPLE SHOWS.** In a policy process, knowledge travels along communication channels. This example shows knowledge moving from sustainable agriculture advocates' position statements and policy briefs into legislation. Bill drafters appropriately transferred from advocacy documents to legislative provisions concepts such as risk-based hazard analysis and domain-specific wording such as "roadside stands" and "farmers markets." This example forcefully reminds us that problem definitions predict solutions, that problems are defined in words, and that word choices matter.

## Summary and Preview

This chapter tells you that problem definition is fundamental in policy work. Here you learn to define problems as an advocate with rhetorical awareness. Next, in chapter 4, you will learn to define problems as a policy analyst with critical awareness of policy discourse.

## References

Bardach, E. 2011. *A practical guide for policy analysis: The eightfold path to more effective problem solving.* 4th ed. Washington, DC: CQ Press.

Garner, Diane L., and Diane H. Smith. 1993. *The complete guide to citing government information resources: A manual for writers and librarians.* Rev. ed. Bethesda, MD: Congressional Information Service.

Kingdon, J. 2003. *Agendas, alternatives, and public policies,* 2ed. New York: Addison-Wesley Educational Publishers Inc.

Stone, Deborah. 2002. *Policy paradox: The art of political decision making,* Rev. ed. New York: W.W. Norton & Company.

## Further Reading

Coplin, W. D. 2007. *The Maxwell manual for good citizenship: Public policy skills in action.* Croton-on-Hudson, NY: Policy Studies Association.

# Evaluation: Analyze and Advise

## Key Concepts

- analyzing policy solutions
- critically analyzing policy discourse

From the perspective of the policy cycle, defining a problem is not solving it. Problem definition comes first in the cycle. Next comes analysis and evaluation of alternatives, whether alternative definitions or alternative solutions. From analysis and evaluation come conclusions, which might lead to recommendations for policy makers. This chapter says that critical thinking and critical awareness of policy discourse are fundamental to analytic know-how.

As it is used here, "critical" generally means a questioning approach to discovery and a skeptical attitude toward conventional wisdom. "Policy discourse" refers broadly to discussion, debate, politics, and procedural communications in governance; it refers narrowly to uses of language in a particular policy process such as the initiative to reform food supply safety (chapter 3). Critical discourse analysis is about inferring the connections of things based on examination of language use (Fairclough 1985). It critiques explicit and implicit language uses to discover connections between texts and their social, cultural, and political contexts. It focuses on ways that power is constructed and on communication's role in its construction and exercise. For instance, by looking critically at the language of political argumentation, critical discourse analysis can uncover ideological perspectives, expose faulty or misleading arguments, and pinpoint information gaps.

65

"Policy analysts need to have well-developed critical abilities" in addition to technical abilities and people skills, one analyst says (Mintrom 2012, p. 22). He remarks that "Policy analysts are at their best when they question the proposals being put forward by others, when they take time to discover why problems are being presented in specific ways, what their sources are, and why they have arisen at this time..." (pp. 20–21).

Critical thinking functions throughout the formation of a policy communicator's knowledge, perspective, position, adaptation, and documentation (Viewpoint 3, chapter 2). Primarily, it functions in the formation of perspective. In the visual arts, where the concept derives, perspective pulls together a viewpoint, features of objects, and horizon to frame a representation of reality such as a landscape. In language arts, perspective similarly directs the representation and interpretation of information. Written or spoken representations of reality generally come to us already framed or presented and interpreted in accordance with a perspective (Graumann 2002). In policy communication, problem definition is an example. As noted in chapter 3, one constituency's problem is another's acceptable status quo. Perspective affects the difference. Another example is policy analysis, where the questions and the analytic approaches form a perspective. For instance, market analysis and comparative institution analysis take different perspectives on a problem. Consequently, each represents the problem differently. Always, perspective is substantive, intrinsic, built in. It is not (usually) consciously intentional. Sometimes, however, it is intentional, even unethical. Perspective can lead communicators to "spin" information or present selectively. "Spin" shapes perception while omitting important counterpoints. Going further, intentional perspective can sometimes drive outright deception.

Telling the difference between normal perspective, "spin," and deception can be hard. That's where critical analysis of discourse can help. For policy evaluators, discovery of perspective is basic "recognition work" (Gee 1999, p. 20). Critical thinking skills for discovering perspective, whether your own perspective or another, are widely taught in this guide. You will find critical thinking tips specific to the focus of each chapter. For instance, in chapter 3, you discover perspective built into problem definition by the exercise of describing a problem from different actors' viewpoints (Task 1). Here in chapter 4, critical thinking and language awareness are taught by several devices: a sketch of critical reading experience, a case of critical discourse analysis performed in a public hearing, a writing sample illustrating a student's use of viewpoint-switching (Example 2), and commentaries highlighting features of samples that exhibit critical thought.

Here's a sketch of critical reading: Early on in reading a document, you begin to infer and to query the communication situation. You ask yourself, "Who is providing this information? To whom? Why?" You look analytically at text features, asking, "What is the message? How is it supported? Any gaps? Why?" You notice that you are attending to what the presentation says directly as well as indirectly, asking, "What is this in reference to? Where is it coming from?" What's its story? Why? Why now?" You might notice how you feel about the communication, asking, "Do I believe this? Do I trust it?"

Critical reading to connect a text with its contexts is different from reading to mine it for relevance to your practical information needs (chapter 2). This sketch imagines workaday critical reading that any policy actor should do.

An actual case of critical discourse analysis performed by a policy analyst testifying as an expert witness in a governmental public hearing is presented next here. Extracts from the hearing's transcript are shown, with information provided on access to the full transcript.

## Case: "Agroterrorism, the Threat to America's Breadbasket"

### November 19, 2003, Hearing by the Senate Government Affairs Committee

Following adoption of the Bioterrorism Act of 2002, legislative committees wanting to extend it proposed new bills and held hearings. Republican Senator Susan Collins of Maine chaired a hearing on proposed amendments extending the 2002 Act to cover agriculture and food industries. In her statement opening the hearing, Senator Collins defines the problem, vulnerability of the U.S. food supply chain. As evidence, she cites a "paper trail" of documentation that she says indicates terrorist intentions to attack the supply chain.

**Opening Statement by Senator Collins, Committee Chair**
"...Hundreds of pages of U.S. agricultural documents recovered from the al Qaeda caves in Afghanistan early last year are a strong indication that terrorists recognize that our agriculture and food industry provides tempting targets. According to a new RAND Corporation report, which will be released at today's hearing, the industry's size, scope, and productivity, combined with our lack of preparedness, offer a great many points of attack. Among our witnesses today will be the report's author, Dr. Peter Chalk, a noted expert in biowarfare....A CIA report...confirmed that the September 11 hijackers expressed interest in crop dusting aircraft....This horrific page is from *The Poisoner's Handbook*, an underground pamphlet published here in the United States that provides detailed instructions on how to make powerful plant, animal, and human poisons from easily obtained ingredients and how to disseminate them. It was found in Afghanistan....Last spring, a Saudi cleric who supports al Qaeda...issued a fatwa, a religious ruling, that justified the use of chemical and biological weapons, including weapons that destroy tillage and stock" [*Agroterrorism*, pp. 1–2].

**Testimony by Peter Chalk, Witness.** The second witness, Peter Chalk, is a risk analyst for the research organization Rand Corporation. He authored the Rand report on biological warfare and agriculture cited by the committee chair in her opening statement. His testimony complicates the discourse she has initiated. Chalk makes measured acknowledgement of the validity of claims made by Collins. However, he qualifies the risk. "Now, although vulnerability does not translate to risk and there are few reported actual incidents of terrorists employing biological agents against agriculture, a realistic potential for such a contingency certainly exists" [p. 14]. He applies probabilistic reasoning to control inferences. "The problem is that you can't extrapolate [a single disease outbreak] to the general agricultural industry because the referent...experience is not there" [p. 22].

Chalk then draws attention to the constructed nature of the threat to food production by showing its inadequate risk assessment. "...I have only come up with two documented cases of the...use of biological weapons deliberately as a political strategy against livestock" [p. 31].

Chalk goes on to rank the risk comparatively. "Despite the ease by which agricultural terrorism can be carried out and the potential ramifications....I don't think that it is likely to constitute a primary form of terrorist aggression....However, I think [such attacks] could certainly emerge as a favored secondary form of aggression..." [p. 17].

Without referring directly to the Rand report that he authored, Chalk effectively disassociates its findings from the "paper trail" in which Senator Collins places it. By resisting the committee chair's frame for the report, he controls the use of his knowledge, perspective, and position in this public process.

(The full transcript can be found at http://frwebgate.access.gpo.gov/ cgi-bn/getdoc.cfh?dbname=108_senate_hearings&docid=f:91045. wais)

---

•➡• **WHAT THIS CASE SHOWS.** The committee chair's opening statement shows faulty cause and effect reasoning and ideological bias (Smith 2009). It purposefully develops a framing perspective, terror. While, as member of the majority political party, and committee chair, Senator Collins has authority and power to frame discussion of food security in relation to the "war on terror, " she does so misleadingly in this hearing. She frames information as terror-related by means of linguistic devices of assembled meaning and recontextualization. Assembled meaning is meaning-by-aggregation, or a constructed association of items. This device relies on many-to-one reduction that sweeps unlike items into one category. The association is not inherent; rather, it is constructed in communication. In her opening statement, Senator Collins purposefully implies a commonality among disparate items. Each is thereby recontextualized and given new meaning by association. While recontextualization is inevitable in discussion, it should not mislead as Senator Collins' constructed association does.

The witness Chalk's rhetorical accomplishment is to deconstruct the association. He dissents without disagreeing. His testimony critiques the chair's position and the terror perspective. Politely, he exposes misleading cause and effect association while agreeing that a problem might exist. He addresses the potential problem analytically. His testimony and answers to questions—distinguishing between vulnerability and risk, measuring the probability of risk, declining to speculate beyond available evidence—show him critically analyzing the policy discourse. His critique draws attention to the terror perspective, making it visible and showing its limits. Politely, the witness constructs alternatives. Effectively, he makes room for debate.

## How to Analyze Policy and Policy Discourse

A problem is recognized. Policy alternatives for addressing it are under consideration. You are asked or you wish to present a definition of the problem and a review of policy alternatives. Your intended audience might be policy makers, an interested community, or the general public. Your strategy is to analyze, both critically and technically. (Note: The task outline of questions assumes that you are prepared to perform—outside the tasks listed here—appropriate technical policy analysis.)

*Goal*: Policy evaluation.
*Objectives*: Consider alternative problem definitions including influential contextual factors. Construct alternative policy responses. Analyze their likely impacts. Critique their descriptive representations. Draw conclusions and offer recommendations.
*Product*: Short or longer written document that can be easily summarized for oral presentation. Length may vary from 1 to 50 or more pages.
*Scope*: Local or broader in impact; widely discussed or ignored; past, present, or anticipated.
*Strategy*: Analyze the discourse. Analyze policy alternatives.

### Task #1. Identify the problem and the stakeholders.

- What is the problem? What brings it to attention? Who brings it to attention?

- Why does the problem come to attention now? What conditions led to the problem?

- Whose behavior is affected, or whose concerns are relevant? Who will benefit by solutions to the problem? Who will pay? Who will implement policy to solve it?
- What stake does each interested party (affected groups, target beneficiaries, implementers of policy) have in the problem?
- How does each define the problem?
- What ideals and values (equity, liberty, efficiency, security, loyalty) or ideologies (vision of how the world is or how it should be) are expressed in each definition?
- What conflicts of values or ideologies are evident among definitions?
- How does politics influence the problem?

## Task #2. Specify alternative solutions and relevant criteria for evaluating them.

- What are the goals/objectives of a public policy to solve this problem?
- What policy instruments might achieve the goals/objectives?
- What are at least two (alternative) policies to meet the need?
- What are the relevant criteria for choosing the best one? How do stakeholders weigh the criteria? How appropriate are the weights? What are the trade-offs among criteria?
- What would be the outcome of each alternative according to criteria you consider relevant?

## Task #3. Recommend an alternative and explain your reasoning (if you are making a recommendation).

- Which policy option or instrument do you recommend? Why is it best? Why are other alternatives worse?
- What is the basis for your recommendation? What type of analysis supports it?
- How will your choice affect stakeholders?
- On what conditions (political, economic, organizational) does successful implementation of your choice depend?
- What are the constraints (political, economic, organizational) on implementing your choice?

## Task #4. Write the document: policy analysis with (or without) recommendation.

Before you write, consider your readiness from the process-into-product viewpoint. Use the Method to consider the communication situation rhetorically and to plan your communication. After you write, use the checklists to assess the product and revise as needed (chapter 2).

Policy analysis is communicated in varied document types. If a particular type is prescribed for you, use it in accordance with your intended purpose and audience. Academic courses might prescribe a policy analysis memo, for instance. If you are free to choose, you might use a memo, a brief statement of position, or an extensive discussion paper.

Policy analyses in any form are expected to do the following:

- characterize a problem according to its size, scope, incidence, effects, perceptions of it, and influences on it
- identify policy choices available to address the problem and the criteria for choosing
- offer perspectives to assist choice
- specify the basis for selecting any proposed recommendation (the type of analysis performed), the effects for different groups, and the factors that will affect its implementation

You must cite the sources to which your policy analysis refers. Use the citation style prescribed, or choose either the APA style (http://www.apastyle.org/learn/faqs/index.aspx) or the MLA style (http://www.mla.org/style). Both APA and MLA style guides tell you how to cite a range of source types, including government documents. (For instance, see *Citing Government Information Sources Using MLA Style* at http://knowledgecenter.unr.edu/help/manage/government_cite.aspx.) For more help, consult Garner and Smith's *The Complete Guide to Citing Government Information Resources: A Manual for Writers and Librarians* (rev. ed.).

# Three Examples

## *Example 1*

Previously you read that a coalition of sustainable agriculture interest groups advocated principles to guide reform (Scenario 2, Example 4, chapter 3). Here, you will read selected recommendations derived from those principles. (You may wish to review Scenario 2, chapter 3 before reading the recommendations here.)

## National Sustainable Agriculture Coalition Policy Brief and Recommendations
## Food Safety on the Farm
October 2009

### Principles and Policy Recommendations

There is no question that our food system needs to be safer. But if proposed food safety legislation and administrative actions are to have the desired effect of reducing pathogen risks and increasing agricultural innovation, long term sustainability, consumer choice, and availability of fresh, high quality produce, they should reflect the following principles and recommendations.

[Principle] I. Measures of safety should be risk-based, focused on risk reduction, and be justified by scientific research.

Proposed regulations and updated GAP guidelines should focus on the highest risk activities. Several areas of concern are highlighted here:

*Centralized Processing.*

Attention should be given to the scale of the food production enterprise and its potential to distribute products to millions of people. In most of the recent outbreaks of food borne illness, the main source of the problem was centralized processing, distribution, and retail distribution, not growing and harvesting.

Centralized processing and distribution means that a single lapse can sicken a large, geographically dispersed set of individuals. Most documented cases of contamination of fresh produce can be traced to processing facilities where the products from multiple farms are commingled. Leafy greens provide an example. The vast majority of "ready to eat" bags of salads, spinaches, lettuces, and lettuce hearts have unique risks associated with them. In the last ten years, 98.5% of all E. coli illnesses originating in California were traced to processed, bagged salad mixes, not to crops harvested as whole heads, bunched greens, or greens that are cooked.

*Manure Use*

Properly composted manure is an effective and safe fertilizer. A great volume of research has shown that judicious use of composted or aged manure is essential for maintaining the high soil microbial diversity and biological activity that is vital to soil quality. The buffering or exclusionary role of diverse microbial communities in soils richer in organic matter has been shown to accelerate die-off of E. coli 0157 and plant pathogens in soil. New safety guidelines, standards, and marketing agreements need not regulate all forms of manure use, but should focus on uncomposted or improperly composted manure, and biosolids, which pose a greater contamination risk. The food safety measures in the National Organic Program include rules for compost, uncomposted manure and biosolids, and may be used as an example.

### Animals of Proven Significant Risk

Food safety guidelines, standards, and marketing agreements should use the term "animals of proven significant risk," instead of referring to all animals or all wildlife when managing risk. Wild animals do not present a significant contamination risk for produce. Preliminary results released in April from a two-year study by the CA wildlife agency, UC Davis, and USDA found that less than one-half of 1 percent of 866 wild animals tested positive for E. coli 0157:H7 in Central California. Unnecessary control or elimination of wildlife could have devastating impacts on the ecosystems surrounding farms. Robust studies also document that deer are not a significant risk. Therefore deer should be eliminated from this list of potential vectors by the California Leafy Greens Marketing Agreement (LGMA).

Instead, new guidelines, standards, and marketing agreements should recognize the relative risk posed by cattle. Studies show that cattle are the primary source of E. coli H7: 0157 with up to 50% of some herds being contaminated. This is particularly true for grain-fed cattle. More research is needed to provide scientific evidence for the sources and vectors of E. Coli H7:0157 and other microbial pathogens to determine if other animals should be deleted or added to the list. Food safety standards should also encourage conservation measures such as perennial forage, buffer strips, and grasses to filter out contamination in overland water flows from livestock feedlots, loafing yards, pastures, and manure storage areas. Emphasis should be placed on halting avenues of contamination between animals and produce fields, including irrigation water contaminated by run-off from feedlots.

### Human Transmission

Experts say that "deficient employee training" is the top food safety problem in the food processing industry.

If employees are not properly trained to implement food safety measures, and if hygiene standards are not enforced, unadulterated products will be at risk for contamination.

*Water Quality*
Quality of irrigation and rinsing water is intimately linked with produce contamination. Irrigation water can become contaminated by nearby large-scale livestock operations or by overflows from sewage systems. Contamination of produce can also stem from the water used to wash produce in processing facilities. FDA must set standards at the processing level to keep water baths from spreading microorganisms among different batches of produce.

## Policy Recommendations:

- In developing guidelines and standards, the FDA and USDA should target critical [high risk] control points in the food system, including processing and packaging, the nature of the supply chain (e.g. the number of steps between the farmgate and end-consumer), that have been documented to increase risk.

- Target FDA and USDA research funding to the most critical [highest risk] points of risk in the food system for fresh produce and other raw agricultural commodities; in processing plants, on water testing of farms; on testing other vectors including animals, people, and dust; on the impact on risk of conservation and biodiversity measures; and on the environmental and social impact on farming of any proposed new food safety measures.

- Additional research should be conducted into the role of resource conservation and soil improvement practices, such as vegetated buffers, and maintaining high soil biological activity and diversity, in reducing on-farm risks of food-borne pathogens in produce fields.

- Protect wildlife and biodiversity by focusing on animals of significant risk, rather than indiscriminate animal control as the FDA and the USDA develop produce guidelines, standards, and marketing agreements.

- Focus safety guidelines, standards, and marketing agreements related to manure on biosolids and uncomposted manure, or improperly composted manure.

- Updated Good Agricultural Practices (GAP) should include recommendations for how to select and use water sources and guidance for producers on how to test water quality at specified intervals.

- Standards should encourage conservation practices that promote food safety.

...

[Principle] VIII. Marketing Agreements and Orders should not be used to regulate food safety.

Food safety should be treated as a pre-competitive area that is not subject to commercial competition. As such, it should not be regulated through the federal office in charge of "facilitating the strategic marketing of agricultural products in domestic and international markets"— the mission of the USDA's Agricultural Marketing Service. Marketing agreements and orders are industry-driven and do not have in place a democratic or transparent process for the development of standards and metrics that will ultimately impact all producers in the respective sector. The members of boards and committees in charge of developing the auditing metrics that are the basis of food safety inspections are appointed, not elected, so the producers signing onto a marketing agreement have to trust that the rules and metrics developed will not be prejudicial or preferential because individuals not necessarily representing them will be drafting laws that affect them.

Policy Recommendation:

- Oppose the proposed national Leafy Greens Marketing Agreement.

(The complete brief and all recommendations can be found at http://sustainableagriculture.net/wp-content/uploads/2008/08/NSAC-Food-Safety-Policy-Brief-October-2009.pdf.)

———

•—• **WHAT THIS EXAMPLE SHOWS.** Critically analyzed in a political context, these recommendations express the perspective of a minority community, a coalition of groups representing sustainable agriculture farmers in the national industry of food growing and handling. The minority perspective sees alternatives to the proposals offered by the majority or representatives of conventional farmers. For instance, the coalition explicitly critiques and opposes a proposal made by an agriculture trade association to reform food supply safety by market management. (The proposed Federal Leafy Greens Marketing Agreement is Example 3 in chapter 7.)

Analyzed as the communication of a perspective, this coalition's recommendations manifest knowledge, position, adaptation, and documentation (Viewpoint 3, chapter 2).

Knowledge or domain familiarity is shown in the dense detail. The language of sustainable agriculture evident in position statements and policy briefs (Examples 3 and 4, chapter 3) and in legislative bill language (Example 5, chapter 3) is recontextualized here in policy evaluation.

Recommendations tailored to the recipients' authority to act show adaptation. In this brief intended for congressional committee members, recommended actions target (some of) what a legislature does—regulate, fund, authorize programs, and oversee administration.

The coalition's position is stated explicitly and argued logically. While logic functions globally in this text to support coherence, it also functions locally to support specific claims. That is, when a thinker-writer claims that something is true, the reader expects supporting evidence. To be taken seriously, positional arguments must exhibit support for claims made. In this example, claims and evidence are tightly linked. Here is an instance:

> The vast majority of "ready to eat" bags of salads, spinaches, lettuces, and lettuce hearts have unique risks associated with them [claim]. In the last ten years, 98.5% of all E.coli illnesses originating in California were traced to processed, bagged salad mixes, not to crops harvested as whole heads, bunched greens, or greens that are cooked [support].

Presentation in this example has two strengths, global coherence of the whole document and clarity of individual sentences. Readers find written text coherent if it motivates them to read carefully and if it lets them know what to expect so that they can read knowledgeably (Williams and Colomb 2012, pp. 107–08).

Multiple devices are used here to motivate and to guide readers. For instance, the tactic of listing aids memory. First introduced to a bare-bones list of principles in the brief's summary (Example 4, chapter 3), readers reencounter the principles in the recommendations. Here, each principle, or "old" information, is listed again, followed by "new" information or recommendations. The old-to-new pattern within a list framework is repeated for eight principles, each having up to five related recommendations. Because the content is specialized and densely detailed with numerous key points, readers' attention might falter without strong guidance by the presenter. Here, readers are helped to attend carefully and knowledgeably by the listing framework and the recurring old-to-new pattern. Whether they hunt for target content or read the entire document, readers are likely to feel confident that the presenter wants them to understand and to care about the subject. Readers trust such presenters.

Presentation is clear at the level of individual sentences. The sentence is an important feature in this document's design for communicating. For instance, each principle is stated as a single sentence. Also, each recommendation is stated as a single sentence. If the sentence is long, its construction is (usually) understandable. Sentences are most clear when the main character is the subject, and the most important action is the verb (Williams and Colomb 2012, p. 9). Other attributes of clarity are exhibited when there are no long introductions at the start of a sentence, and no interruptions between the subject and verb. Clarity is enhanced, too, by varying the length of sentences. A short sentence following long sentences offers relief. The following instance shows a clearly constructed long sentence and a short sentence following it. Italics have been added for emphasis.

> Most documented *cases* [subject] of contamination of fresh produce *can be traced* [verb] to processing facilities where the products from multiple farms are commingled. Leafy greens provide an example.

In other instances, long sentences are less clear because they have too many characters and actions. They might also have a long introduction. Consequently, focus is weakened. Here is an illustration:

> **Original.** In *developing* guidelines and standards [action], the *FDA and USDA* [characters] *should target* [action] critical [meaning high-risk] control points in the food system, including *processing and packaging* [action as character], the *nature of the supply chain* [character] (e.g. the number of steps between the farmgate and end-consumer), that have been *documented* [action] to *increase* risk [action].

Readers might get lost in such action-packed sentences. As a remedy, this long sentence could be divided into two sentences, each with a single main character and action or subject and verb. The first sentence's introduction could be eliminated. The action of the first sentence could become the character of the next, for coherence. Here's how:

> **Revision**. *FDA and USDA guidelines and standards* [character] *should target* [action] critical [meaning high-risk] control points in the food system. *Targets* [character] *should include* [action] documented causes of risk such as processing and packaging, the nature of the supply chain (e.g., the number of steps between the farmgate and the end-consumer).

For more instruction in revising sentences as shown here, see guides by Williams and Colomb (2012) and Smith (1987) referenced at the end of this chapter.

## Example 2

To fill a course assignment, a graduate student in public policy communication wrote a policy brief with recommendation. At the time, she was also a career professional in a federal administrative agency. For the academic assignment, she chose to evaluate policies pertaining to a familiar subject from her professional work, aviation noise. To communicate her policy evaluation and recommendation, she adopted the persona of a concerned citizen representing a homeowner association affected by the problem. The homeowners live near a large airport. In her professional work, she often interacted with similar civic associations. She took that persona for the assignment to discover perspective, as an exercise in critical analysis. She wanted to see the problem from an affected population's viewpoint rather than from her own agency administrator's viewpoint.

### MEMORANDUM

*To:* Representative Howard Coble (R-NC), Transportation and Infrastructure Committee

*From:* John Johns, Esquire, President, Ebenezer Homeowners' Association (EHA)

*SUBJ:* Briefing Memo to Define the Problem: Aviation Noise Pollution Poses an Increased Risk to our Nation's Health that Requires Immediate Federal Oversight

***Date:*** March 14, 2011

***cc:*** Armando Tovar, Noise Officer, Raleigh-Durham Airport (RDU) Authority

Greg Denning and Tim McBrayer, Wake County Members of the Raleigh-Durham Noise Committee

## OVERVIEW

Noise pollution presents an increasing danger to the health and welfare of our Nation's population. One of the major sources of noise pollution is the aviation industry. Air transportation has become the predominant mass transportation system in the United States. As the aviation industry expands so does the harmful impact of noise pollution on our population.

Control of aviation noise primarily rests with state and local governments as a result of public law shifting responsibility away from federal government. This has contributed to inconsistencies in aviation noise control and abatement policies across the nation. As a result, major gaps exist in protective coverage of all its citizens from noise pollution.

A study is needed now to determine the feasibility of assigning aviation noise control and abatement to the federal level. The Federal Aviation Administration (FAA) currently receives funding for aviation noise control and abatement. FAA's role to support the economic expansion of the aviation industry is in direct conflict with public protection from aviation noise pollution. Specifically, consideration should be given to funding the Environmental Protection Agency's (EPA) Office of Noise Abatement and Control (ONAC) to set national policy and implement standards uniformly.

## POSITION

*Studies Emerge on the Harmful Impact of Aviation Noise on Health*
Our nation's health is at risk. According to the World Health Organization's Guidelines for Community Noise, noise is a major, increasing health risk factor. Adverse health effects from noise include hearing loss; sleep disturbances; cardiovascular and psycho-physiologic problems; performance reduction; annoyance responses; and adverse social behavior (1).

*Public Awareness of Aviation Noise as a Pollutant*
Aircraft noise first began to draw attention as an annoyance in the late 1960s. As the increase in aviation noise rose in the 1970s and 1980s, it became a greater concern to those living in close proximity

to airports. In the 1970s, with the creation of the EPA's Office of Noise Abatement and Control (ONAC) attention was brought to the fact that aviation noise was a pollutant rather than simply an annoyance. The Quiet Communities Act of 1978 mandated research in noise control, education programs and the establishment of the Quiet Communities Program (2). This remains in effect today providing limited relief to select communities.

### EPA and FAA Shared Oversight Ineffective
During the 1970s, EPA was to recommend noise standards to FAA based on consideration of public health and welfare. FAA was to determine if the proposed EPA standards were consistent with safety, economically reasonable and technologically practical to implement and enforce. During the 1970s, the FAA focused on a new problem in aviation, that of terrorists hijackings. In the 1980s, FAA dealt with the nationwide strike of Air Traffic Controllers with the demand to rebuild a new workforce. With the aftermath of September 11, 2001, the FAA worked to restore confidence in air transportation. Now, FAA turns its focus on the replacement of outdated air traffic control technology. All plausible reasons that the FAA did not aggressively tackle noise abatement as its top priority.

### State and Local Oversight Applied Inconsistently
In 1981, under the Reagan Administration, EPA's ONAC ceased to be funded. The thought was that noise abatement would be best addressed at the state and local levels. This resulted in inconsistencies in the oversight of aviation noise and abatement from community to community. New technology exists for quieter aircraft, appropriate land use surrounding airports, sound proofing techniques, barrier construction and acoustical shields to reduce noise and they should be applied uniformly. Without national, uniform noise control and abatement standards, our entire population is not protected adequately against the health hazards of aviation noise pollution.

### Noise Measurement to Assess Aviation Noise Inadequate
It is acknowledged that the Day-Night Level (DNL) is not the best tool to use since it uses an average of noise levels of all aircraft that land and depart in a 24-hour period. According to one FAA expert, "The DNL is really not a good metric but it is the best anyone has developed" (3). This tool should measure single event noise and sustained background noise levels. Studies indicate that noise is a hazard at 50 decibels and higher. The FAA uses 65 decibels and higher to monitor noise. FAA contends that only an estimated 500,000 people

nationwide are directly impacted by aviation noise using the 65 decibels (4). Estimates by citizen's groups estimate the number of people
at risk occur in the millions nationally based on citizen complaints. One
estimate of the Chicago O'Hare Airport area alone, estimates that 1.6
million people are adversely affected by noise pollution (5).

*Legislative History Indicates Limited Focus on Aviation Noise*
The Noise Control Act of 1972 was an initial step to involve EPA in
the regulation of aircraft noise. EPA recommended noise standards to
FAA based on considerations of public health and welfare (6). EPA's
mission for the protection of human health and the environment places
EPA as the more appropriate agency for oversight. FAA focused on the
promotion of the aviation industry and not on public health or welfare.
This is evident in its criteria to restrict Stage 3 aircraft noise that mandates any airport restriction must:

- be reasonable, non-arbitrary and non-discriminatory,
- not create an undue burden on interstate or foreign commerce,
- be consistent with safe and efficient use of navigable airspace,
- not conflict with any existing federal statutes or regulation, and
- not create an undue burden on the national aviation system (7).

## VARIOUS VIEWPOINTS

The Ebenezer Homeowners' Association recognizes the economic
value of the Raleigh-Durham (RDU) Airport. Annually, RDU generates revenue of $2 billion and supports 6,000 jobs (8). EHA also
understands that noise is inherent in the operation of aircraft. The
association thinks that existing measures currently exist to significantly reduce the adverse impact of noise in the surrounding area.

The aircraft and aviation industry view aviation noise control and
abatement as an expensive cost of doing business. Costs are inherent in developing quieter aircraft technology or retrofitting current aircraft. The costs to citizen's health and welfare must also be
considered.

The RDU Airport Authority attempts "to balance the demand for
increased services with the concerns of communities around the airport" (8). However, aircraft are allowed to access the airport anytime
of day or night. Communities nationwide require federal oversight

to focus on measures that protect the population against dangerous levels of aviation noise.

The FAA points out that the worst levels of noise in the 70–75 DNL range have been removed. The removal of Stage 1 and Stage 2 aircraft contributed significantly to this reduction. However, the FAA uses noise at 65 DNL or higher, as its target level for noise reduction. This may have been a good initial target to reduce from 75 DNL but it does not come close to the 50 DNL or higher range that causes adverse health and welfare issues (9). The aviation industry is expected to grow along with the byproduct of increased noise pollution. The population remains at risk.

---

## ►•  SOURCES CITED.

1. World Health Organization (WHO), *Guidelines for Community Noise*, April 1999, World Health Organization, Geneva, Switzerland, http://www.who.int/environmental_information_information/noise/Comnoise6.htm (Edited by Birgitta Berglund, Thomas Lindvall, and Dietrich H. Schwela)

2. U.S. Senate, 95th Congress, 2nd Session (1978), S. 3083: *The Quiet Communities Act*, Online: Thomas.loc.gov. 14 February 2011. http://thomas.loc.gov/cgi-bin/dbquery/z?do95: SN03083:‖TOM:/bss/do95query.html‖, (Public Law 95–609).

3. Email dated 18 February 2011, Subject: *Noise*, from Scott Seritt, Manager, Atlanta Airports District Office (contact: Scott.Seritt@faa.gov).

4. Federal Aviation Administration's *2010 Business Plan*, October 15, 2009, (Flight Plan Target: Noise exposure) www.faa.gov

5. Public comment from US Citizens Aviation Watch Association and the Alliance of Residents Concerning O'Hare to the Federal Aviation Administration's public call for comment to revise the *1976 National Aviation Noise Abatement Policy*, October 20, 2000.

6. *Noise Control Act*, 42 U.S.C. § 401 et seq., (1972). Online: General Services Administration, 9 February 2011. http://www.

gsa.gov/graphics/pbs/Noise_Control_Act_ of 1972.pdf, (Public Law 92–574).

7. Federal Aviation Administration's Federal Aviation Regulations Part 161, *Notice and Approval of Airport Noise and Access Restrictions* dated September 25, 1991, http://www.faa.gov

8. Raleigh-Durham Airport Authority, *RDU Aircraft Noise Program*, 10 March 2011. Online: http://www.rduaircraftnoise. com/noiseinfo/managegrowth.html

9. *Report on Noise*. U.S. Environmental Protection Agency, U.S. Government Printing Office, December 31, 1971, Washington, DC.

---

**What This Example Shows.** Critical thinking is shown in Example 2 by the comparison of alternative viewpoints. Equal consideration is given to each viewpoint, demonstrating a perspective of fairness. Detailed familiarity with the domain indicates a knowledgeable policy analyst. Information is adapted to the intended reader, a committee chair with authority to act. This memo might serve well to brief officials or their staff members (chapter 8). It is written documentation that could easily translate to key points for oral briefing.

Critical analysis of policy discourse is evident here in the critique of positions taken by administrative agencies over time. Policy positions are described as products of their historical and political context, as a way of showing their limitations. This critique of precedents' limitations helps to specify current needs for reform.

As documentation, the example skillfully uses organizational devices such as subheadings to motivate informed reading and to serve rapid reading. Typically, sentences are constructed well to bear their load of detail. Occasionally, the presenter misses an opportunity to use storytelling to motivate readers' understanding of the homeowners' position. Here is an instance:

> With the aftermath of September 11, 2001, the FAA worked to restore confidence in air transportation. Now, FAA turns its focus on the replacement of outdated air traffic control

technology. All plausible reasons that the FAA did not aggressively tackle noise abatement as its top priority.

The final sentence occupies an important position in the paragraph. Recipients expect last sentences to cue knowledgeable reading by summarizing or repeating key points. If this final sentence were revised as follows, recipients would be reminded of the memo's recommendation to transfer noise abatement authority from the FAA to the EPA. "These shifting FAA's priorities over a decade explain, but do not justify, its unaggressive approach to noise abatement." The revision would also silently remedy a grammatical error, the original fragmentary sentence's lack of subject and verb.

## Example 3

This sample was originally written for a think tank as a report of academic research on taxation as social policy, with a focus on taxes paid by low-wage workers (Gitterman 2003). The report was revised in 2007, partly on request by a legislator, as a policy brief with recommendations intended for policymakers, with a focus on the earned income tax credit (EITC). That brief is publicly available on the authors' university research center website, and it is sampled here. A further revision is published in a scholarly journal (Gitterman et al., 2008).

The brief's evaluation of policy options and a recommendation are shown here. Other parts are shown in chapter 5 (Example 3) and chapter 6.

### Expanding the EITC for Single Workers and Couples Without Children

### (aka Tax Relief for Low-Wage Workers)

Daniel P. Gitterman, Lucy S. Gorham, Jessica L. Dorrance
A Discussion Paper prepared for the Center on Poverty, Work and Opportunity at the University of North Carolina at Chapel Hill

**January 2007**

...

Analysis and Policy Proposals
*Policy options to expand the EITC for (or provide additional tax relief to) childless single and married workers*

A number of policy proposals for expansion of the EITC for childless single and married workers have been offered over the past decade....The primary motivations behind these proposals have been to: a) improve tax fairness by mitigating the disproportionate level of taxes paid by single low-wage workers, especially after the tax law changes of the last decade which in many cases have increased the regressivity of the tax code; b) increase this group's attachment to the labor market, as earlier expansions of the EITC have proven to do for low-wage workers with children; and c) reduce the likelihood that workers engaging in significant labor market effort will remain in poverty.

In addition, we discuss three other issues that an expanded EITC for childless single and married workers could potentially address: the need to provide stronger incentives for workforce participation for young workers entering the labor market; high health insurance costs; and the importance of helping all low-income workers build savings and other assets.

In this section, we highlight options for expanding the EITC for single and childless workers, each of which addresses a somewhat different purpose and several of which target specific subgroups of EITC recipients....For each option, we describe its purpose, the policy change needed, the estimated budget impact if available, and complementary policy changes that are desirable.

**1.** EITC Baseline Expansion for Single and Married Childless Couples

The first proposed recommendation with the broadest impact...would increase the EITC to 15.3 percent of earnings to provide relief from payroll and other taxes, doubling the current level of 7.65 percent of earnings. According to estimates by the Center for Budget and Policy Priorities (Furman, 2006), these changes would have an additional budget impact of approximately $3 billion and would increase the maximum EITC benefit for single and married childless workers from $399 to $1,236. Fully offsetting payroll taxes requires an EITC pegged at 15.3 percent of earnings.

...However, we note that by selecting differing percentage figures for the share of earnings that would qualify and using different phase-in and phase-out thresholds, an almost infinite number of variations of this proposal could be designed resulting in higher or lower EITC benefit levels and a correspondingly higher or lower budget impact.

...

**2.** Increased Work Incentives for Younger Workers

In addition to the increased work incentives provided by the baseline EITC expansion proposed above in (1), a second policy recommendation would further increase the incentives for young workers to participate in the legitimate labor market by lowering the age limit at which workers without children can qualify for the EITC from 25 to 21. We view this proposal as an addition to the baseline expansion proposed in (1), which is of higher priority, but it could be instituted independently....No such age requirement applies to workers with children—as long as they are not claimed as a dependent on another taxpayer's return, they may file for the EITC....An analysis of this type of expansion for younger workers offered by Edelman, Holzer, and Offner (2006) includes an estimate of its cost at between $1 billion and $2 billion...

**3.** Expanding available funds for monthly health insurance premiums or retirement plan contributions

A third policy recommendation would assist any worker eligible for the EITC to address the high costs of health care and/or to increase funds available for retirement plan contributions. The health insurance component is particularly relevant to single and childless workers because they are less likely to qualify for Medicaid or the State Children's Health Insurance Program (SCHIP). Workers could enroll in the Advance EITC, which pays low-wage workers an extra amount in their regular paycheck each month. They would then target that Advance EITC to pay a share of their health insurance premium....A similar approach could be used for an employer-based retirement plan, such as a 401(k). As was true for proposal (2) to make childless workers eligible for the EITC beginning at age 21, we view this proposal as working best if it were in addition to a baseline expansion of the EITC since this would increase the funds available for health insurance premiums or retirement contributions.

...

**4.** Helping Childless Workers to Save and Build Assets

...Because [the EITC] can represent a significant amount of money to receive in one payment, it is often used by low and moderate-income families as a way to save money over the year. As generations of experience with traditional welfare has shown, however, a marginal increase in income rarely ends the poverty cycle for a family without some accumulation of assets. Federal policies have long favored the development of assets through tax breaks for 401(k)s, mortgage interest, and small businesses, and initiatives like the GI bill. Unfortunately, most of these policies do not benefit low-income families, who may not earn enough to pay income tax or have access to tax-deferred retirement accounts.

...

An expanded EITC for childless workers has great potential to be an essential component of a more far-reaching initiative to reduce poverty and build assets if we are willing to experiment with and invest in innovative approaches. We propose that the matched savings account concept be expanded so that, in this case, single and childless workers could use the added income from an expanded EITC benefit to invest in savings vehicles such as Individual Retirement Accounts (IRAs), Coverdell Education Savings Accounts (ESAs), and college savings 529 accounts and that their contributions be matched.

...

Lastly, we consider three complementary policy recommendations that would assist savings and asset building initiatives linked to an expanded EITC. The first is to make the Saver's Credit, which Congress recently made permanent, fully refundable so that it is more advantageous to low-income savers. The second calls for Congress to appropriate funding to the IRS to fund community free tax preparation programs for low-income tax filers similar to the funds it has provided for free tax preparation programs for the elderly and military families...

The third, and final, proposal related to expanding opportunities for asset building, is to increase, or eliminate, the asset limits that are attached to a range of public benefit programs and which have a dampening effect on the propensity of public benefit recipients to save....This issue is of particular concern to workers with disabilities since they often must rely on social security and Medicaid.

### Conclusions and Suggestions for Policy Reform

*Putting an EITC for Singles in a Broader Federal Tax Policy Context*

...

Distributional and fairness concerns have always emerged during debates on broader tax policy reform proposals. As part of large congressional reconciliation tax-cut packages, EITC expansions have been used to maintain distributional equity for tax policy reform as a whole...

The simple conclusion of our work is that workers without children who live below the poverty line should *not* be subject to high federal income taxes and taxed deeper into poverty. We hope to begin a dialogue rather than recommend one way to policy reform.

...

The most significant challenge for policymakers, policy researchers and Washington DC think tanks concerned about federal tax relief for low-income single and married couples without children is to continue to generate thoughtful empirical analysis and policy conclusions that show how to make our tax code fair for those workers and non-custodial parents who also work hard and play by the rules. The politics of tax policy research will continue to pose major challenges for research on the distributional implications of tax reform. The key challenge is how the trio of federal individual income tax provisions—personal exemptions, standard deduction, and tax credits—together can shelter a certain amount of earned wages from federal tax liability and thus increase the amount of take-home pay of all low-wage workers. Certainly, the budgetary environment of the moment does not hold a great deal of promise for expanded EITC commitments. Yet, recent political history over the last three decades demonstrates that new or expanded work and family support efforts are indeed possible politically, even at times of budget and economic stress....An expanded EITC for single and childless workers could emerge as a proposal with considerable political traction.

(The policy brief can be found at http://www.law.unc.edu/documents/poverty/publications/gittermanpolicybrief.pdf

Also see Gitterman 2003 and Gitterman, et al. 2008.)

───────

**•━• What This Example Shows.** This publication history illustrates the flow of policy analysis between research and practical politics. As a policy communication, Example 3 demonstrates knowhow, or awareness that policy analysts need the capability of adapting information to the purposes of varied users and of communicating in multiple genres.

This sample's analysis defines a recognized problem, the tax burden of low-wage workers, and recommends a recognized solution, expanding a tax credit.

As a policy communication, the sample demonstrates skill in authoritative argumentation to support the recommendation. (See chapter 6 for examination of the sample's argument.) Its argument exemplifies critical thinking to evaluate policy options, to explore values inherent in the recommended policy instrument, and to identify limitations as well as benefits of utilizing that option. Critical analysis of policy discourse is shown by the brief's claim that tax policy expresses political agendas. The claim is supported by a legislative history tracing policy changes to power shifts in government over time. (See chapter 5 for the sample's summary of legislative history.)

## Summary and Preview

This chapter tells you that analysis is fundamental in policy work. Two kinds of analysis are important, analysis of policy solutions and analysis of policy discourse. To communicate analysis in support of recommendations, skill in argumentation is required. In chapter 5 you'll learn about conducting government records research to develop knowledge and inform your argument. In chapter 6 you'll learn about arguing in political contexts.

## References

*Agroterrorism: The threat to America's breadbasket.* 2004. A hearing before the committee on governmental affairs, U.S. Senate, 108th Congress, 1st session, November 19, 2003. Washington, DC: U.S. Government Printing Office.

Fairclough, Norman. 1985. Critical and descriptive goals in discourse analysis. *Journal of Pragmatics* 9: 739—63.

Garner, D. L., and D. H. Smith. 1993. *The complete guide to citing government information resources: A manual for writers and librarians.* Rev. ed. Bethesda, MD: Congressional Information Service.

Gee, James Paul. 1999. *An introduction to discourse analysis: Theory and method.* London and New York: Routledge.

Gitterman, Daniel P. 2003. Tax credits for working families. http://www.brookings.edu/reports/2003/08childrenfamilies_gitterman.aspx

Gitterman, Daniel P., Lucy S. Gorham, and Jessica L. Dorrance. 2008. Expanding the EITC for single workers and couples without children: Tax relief for all low-wage workers. *Georgetown Journal on Poverty Law and Policy* 15: Number 2, 245—84.

Graumann, Carl F. 2002. Explicit and implicit perspectivity. *Perspective and perspectivity in discourse.* Eds. C.F. Graumann and Werner Kallmeyer. Amsterdam/Philadelphia: John Benjamins Publishing Company.

Mintrom, Michael. 2012. *Contemporary policy analysis.* New York: Oxford University Press.

Smith, Catherine F. 2009. Public professional communication in the antiterror age: A discourse analysis. *Connecting people with technology: Issues in professional communication*, 90–117. Eds. George F. Hayhoe and Helen M. Grady. Amityville, NY: Baywood.

Smith, John B. and Catherine F. Smith. 1987. *A strategic method for writing.* http://www.cs.unc.edu/~jbs/sm

Stone, D. 2002. *Policy paradox: The art of political decision making.* Rev. ed. New York: WW Norton & Company.

Williams, Joseph M. and Gregory C. Colomb. 2012. *Style: The basics of clarity and grace.* 4th ed. Boston: Pearson Longman.

## Further Reading

Bardach, E. 2011. *A practical guide for policy analysis: The eightfold path to more effective problem solving.* 4th ed. Washington DC: CQ Press.

Redman, Eric. 2000. *The dance of legislation.* Seattle: University of Washington Press. [First published in 1973. New York: Simon and Schuster]

# CHAPTER 5

# Legislative History: Know the Record

## Key Concepts

- record of legislative action
- legislative intent

Public policy making requires information about prior government action. This chapter shows you how to research legislative records and to write a legislative history.

Many kinds of information are needed for policy making. To frame a problem, identify its issues, or propose solutions, you might need to know about influential social history, technological developments, and economic patterns. You might consult scientific research, public testimony, advice of expert consultants and lobbyists, statistical data, government agency reports, transcripts of legal proceedings, and more. But one kind of information is essential: the history of government action on the problem. To get that information, you must consult the legislative record; you must be able to conduct legislative research using government documents.

Why is knowledge of the record important? Three reasons. First, for policy making, precedent matters. Action builds on prior action. Knowledge of precedent helps you to frame problems and to find solutions. Second, context matters. The record shows deliberation and debate. Third, content matters. The preamble or the statement of purpose of a published bill or law enables you to discern original intent and the intent of amendments. If you are proposing new action, credibility and standards for policy argument demand that you know the history of prior action.

Who conducts legislative research, and for what purposes? Government staff members (and sometimes interns) consult the legislative record to help them frame problems and identify issues. Outside government, professional staff (and sometimes interns) in organizations of many kinds such as nonprofit groups, trade associations, and policy institutes, consult the record. They do so in order to inform their advocacy or analysis. Similarly, active citizens consult the record as independent researchers. They might pursue a personal interest, or they might volunteer to investigate a record of action that is relevant to an organization's mission. For legal interpretation, court clerks, law librarians, and legal services professionals regularly consult the legislative record to know a law's intent as part of adjudicating disputes over a law's meaning.

Who writes legislative history documents? Often, the people who conduct the research also write the document that reports the results. Government staff or professional researchers on contract to a committee or agency or volunteers for organizations, as well as individuals doing independent research, might produce a legislative history tailored to a particular need to know.

Interns might be assigned these research and writing tasks. To illustrate, a supervisor in a health care policy institute asks an undergraduate intern to specify unmet needs in elder health care for a position paper being written by the institute's director. The supervisor gives no instructions on how to gather the necessary information. The intern considers how to approach the task. She figures that in order to identify unmet needs, she must know what current law provides. As a strategy for getting started, she works from familiar experience. Her elderly grandparents experienced nursing home care, so she decides to start by collecting information on nursing homes.

She goes, first, to the institute's reports published on its website. She finds that they are in-depth analyses of individual laws. Because the website has no index or search engine, she cannot locate laws that refer to nursing homes unless she reads all the reports. She does not have time for that. She then tries searching on the Internet, using an all-purpose search engine and the search term "nursing home care."

That yields advertisements for providers and websites of advocacy groups, but little legislation or public debate. Stymied, she asks the institute's professional staff for help. A policy analyst directs her to government databases and to commercial databases of government information on the Internet. She uses the indexing vocabulary for each database to streamline her searches by emerging topics—first, nursing home care; then hospital care, prescription drugs, and so on. Search results suggest to her that a good time frame to focus on would be the years in office of the previous federal government administration. She searches her favorite government database again in that time frame, and she spends several hours reading summaries of laws and proposed bills. She also checks the final action taken on each.

By the end of the day, she writes a two-page legislative history of elder care. She defines the most pressing current needs to be those that were recognized by the previous administration but left unresolved. She summarizes a list of unmet needs culled from a range of bills or amendments proposed but not passed or adopted. She identifies the most significant failures in elder healthcare proposals (according to criteria that she provides) and distills the public debate surrounding them. In a concluding reference list, she cites these bills or amendments by bibliographic identifiers in the databases so that the institute director can quickly find the acts to read their language. Task accomplished.

## How to Conduct Legislative Research and Write a Legislative History

*Goal*: Knowledge of U.S. proposed or enacted law regarding a defined problem based on consulting legislative records.

*Objective*: Credible reporting of government action.

*Product*: Written document tracing either history of a single law or history of laws on an issue.

*Scope*: Either a single law or an issue involving multiple laws. Relevant action might be at the federal, state, or municipal level, or at several levels. In addition to legislative records, administrative records of rule making and regulation and judicial records of litigation might be needed.

*Strategy*: Multiple approaches are available. No single approach to government records research fits all; however, you will save time and frustration by planning before you start. Use the guidelines given in the following sections to select a strategy.

———

**KNOW WHY THE RESEARCH IS NEEDED.** Legislative uses for the research might be satisfied with past records. In contrast, legal uses might require very current information not yet recorded that only an informant can provide. Knowing the purpose for the research tells you what, and how much, to look for. Will the information be used to make new law (legislative) or to interpret existing law (legal)?

In either case, there might be a published history that meets the purpose. Or you might need to find the records required to write a specialized history. Knowing the purpose for the research can help you (or a librarian assisting you) to decide where to look first. Do you want to find a history or write one?

———

**KNOW THE USER AND THE USER'S PURPOSE FOR THE INFORMATION.** Who, exactly, will use the information, and what is his or her interest or need? The user might be you, gathering information for personal use or for an academic or internship assignment. Or the user for whom you are conducting the research might be a legislator who wants to amend an existing law. Knowing the user's purpose tells you what, and how much, to look for. Federal records only? State or municipal records also?

———

**SET THE SCOPE.** Will the research follow a single law through all its forms and related actions—bill, codified statute, administration, regulation, amendment, and (possibly) adjudication? Or will your research follow an issue through policy changes and across multiple laws over time? What is the relevant time frame? What is the relevant level of government?

---

**➤ TAKE THE NECESSARY TIME, AND MANAGE YOUR TIME.** Records research can take hours, days, or weeks, depending on how much you already know, what you are looking for, where the records are, how well you have planned, and other contingencies. Prepare for the reality that legislative records research will take time, probably more time than you initially planned. What is your deadline for completing the research? What is your schedule for conducting the research and writing the necessary documents?

---

**➤ USE EXISTING SKILLS, AND ADD NEEDED ONES.** If you have a well-defined problem, are willing to learn, are curious and persistent, and have basic research skills including the ability to ask questions, identify relevant sources, and search computer databases, you are basically ready to perform legislative research.

You might need to learn about the legislative process, government record types, and standard tools for researching government records. If so, review as necessary using the tools suggested next here.

### Task #1. Review the Legislative Process

If you already know federal legislative procedure well or if you are tracing state law, omit Task 1 and go on to Task 2.

As you conduct research in government records, you can feel as if you are drowning in information, classification systems, procedure names, and document types. Also, if you start into records searching without knowing the underlying legislative process, you will quickly become lost. Use the following reviews of the process to revive your effort (bookmarking your favorite and returning to it as often as needed):

- The House: How Our Laws Are Made (by House of Representatives Parliamentarian) http://thomas.loc.gov/home/lawsmade.toc.html

- The Senate: Enactment of a Law (by Senate Parliamentarian) http://thomas.loc.gov/home/enactment/enactlawtoc.html
- The Legislative Process http://www.house.gov/content/learn/legislative_process/
- How Does Congress Work? (by Indiana University Center on Congress)     http://congress.indiana.edu/how-does-congress-work
- The Legislative Process (by Congress.org) http://congress.org/congressorg/issues/basics/?style=legis

## Task #2. Conduct Research

Do you want to find a history or write one? Decide early whether your purpose is served by using an already published history or by producing one. For single laws, commercial research services such as the Congressional Information Service publish legislative histories with varying levels of detail. To look for a published history for a single law, try these sources:

- Law Librarians Society of Washington, DC, Legislative Sourcebook http://www.llsdc.org/sourcebook
- CIS/Annual (Year), Legislative Histories of U.S. Public Laws

You are unlikely to find published legislative histories for an issue. Typically, they are specially produced by, or for, users who want the information and tailored to their purposes.

As a general rule, federal records are accessible online and in research libraries. State records are generally less so, but an individual state's records might be available online or, more likely, in the print archives of the state's library. Local government records are generally not available unless you go to the municipality to ask about access to records. Few municipalities put their records online.

Major tools for finding federal and state records are provided by government information services, either free or by subscription. Free services can be accessed from any computer with World Wide Web access. Subscription services are accessed via the Web by authorized users of facilities provided by a subscriber, such as a university library.

From your computer at home and in many public libraries, you can freely access federal records back to 1970 (and link to online state records) through:

- Thomas (Library of Congress) http://thomas.loc.gov
- Government Printing Office (GPO) http://www.gpo.gov/fdsys/

For excellent, comprehensive tips on accessing government records, the following is a good source:

- Frequently Asked Questions at http://thomas.loc.gov/home/faqlist.html

Other free access to numerous federal government websites that link to records is provided by these sources:

- Government Documents Center Reference (University of Michigan Documents Center) http://www.lib.umich.edu/government-documents-center
- Government Documents/Information (Mansfield University) http://mansfield.libguides.com/govdocs
- Catalogue of U.S. Government Publications http://catalog.gpo.gov/F

For state legislatures and local government, these are good websites:

- State and Local Governments (Library of Congress) http://www.loc.gov/rr/news/stategov/stategov.html
- Legal Research (Virtual Chase) http://virtualchase.justia.com/
- Law Librarians Society of Washington, DC, Legislative Sourcebook: State Legislatures, State Laws, State Regulations http://www.llsdc.org/sourcebook

An excellent subscription service used in most university libraries for comprehensive federal legislative information is Lexis-Nexis *Congressional*, based on the (print) *Congressional Information Service (CIS)* documentation. This database is available to subscribers only. You can access it in subscribing research libraries. Free and subscription services are available in federal depository libraries. Those are research libraries, often at colleges and universities, that make GPO materials publicly available in the library's region. Find a depository library near you in the Federal Depository Library Locator at http://catalog.gpo.gov/fdlpdir/FDLPdir.jsp.

Libraries offer a valuable resource: librarians! For professional, skilled, and time-saving assistance in legislative research, always ask a librarian.

*General Tips for Using Government Information Libraries*

- Depository libraries have federal government records in all available forms—digital, print, and microfiche. Depending on what you want to know, you might need all three. Online access to digital records is convenient for recent records, but print and microfiche are still important, too, for several reasons. Records before the 1970s are not yet available online, and some never will be. You can miss a lot of legislative history if you only search online. Also, print compilations are sometimes easier to use, because they are well supplemented by indexes and other locator aids. When using a tool new to you, check first for finding aids, such as an index. You will save much time this way. (Note: Subscription services have more finding aids than do free services.)

- You should take detailed notes as you go. Jot down contextual information and target information. List names of people, committees, subcommittees, and bill or law citations mentioned in the target record. Why? If your first search method fails, these notes can restart your search; they give you alternative ways to search.

You can use what you know to find what you want. For example, if a student intern researching elder health care jots down key terms, citations, names, and dates as she works in a database of government records, she is prepared to search by any of these alternatives:

- by subjects discussed in the record (for example, elder health care)

- by citation (number and letter "addresses") of a particular legislative record in a system of citation, (for example, H.R. 1091–106 for a particular House of Representatives bill)

- by names, dates, committees, or other elements of a legislative process (for example, the name of the senator sponsoring a bill)

In other words, she could find legislation on elder health care by subject (elder health care, nursing home care, Medicare, and so on), or by citation (H.R. 1091–106), or by names or titles in legislative process information (e.g., Senator Tom Harkin; hearing witness Kathleen Sebelius, Department of Health and Human Services; Senate Committee on Health, Education, Labor, and Pensions).

## Task #3. Write the Legislative History Document

To write your legislative history, begin by using the Method in chapter 2. You can reuse the thinking that went into planning your research (see *How to, Strategy,* this chapter). Use it to plan your legislative history document. Let your intended reader's needs for the information guide your selection of information for the history.

What is the message of a legislative history? It is your conclusion formed after consulting the record. The history's scope is set by the purpose (whether you are writing a law history or an issue history) and by the amount of information required to support your message. In any case, you must organize your information to support the message. Organizational options include chronology (to show developments over time), significance (to highlight influential legislation), and trend (to show a pattern).

If no form is prescribed for presenting the results of your research, you might choose to use the following standard reporting format for professional and technical communication:

- overview that concisely summarizes both the message and the key information in the document
- subsections that provide summaries of information
- subheadings that label each subsection
- citations that are provided for each subsection

Citation is very important in a legislative history. The history's credibility and the practical needs of the information user (and the researcher) demand that all sources be easy to locate for confirmation and referral. Citations are the means of doing so. A full citation provides three kinds of information about a source: what type of record it is, how it is classified in a system of documentation, who publishes it (a commercial research service or government). For government records, a full citation includes all the elements that help to identify a source. In legislative research, a full citation, or government style, is preferred over a terse citation, or legal style, that provides only an abbreviated source identifier, number in a system of documentation, and date. If either the government style or legal style is prescribed for you, use that style. If not, choose the appropriate style and use it exclusively. Do not mix styles.

Here is a list of the elements in a full citation, or government style, for citing federal or state legislation:

- issuing agency (house, number, session, year)
- title (document number and name; long name may be abbreviated)
- edition or version
- imprint (city, publisher, date of publication)
- series (serial list of publications)
- notes (in parentheses, add anything not already included in the citation that helps to locate the document)

Following are two illustrations of government style:

1. U.S. House. 101st Congress, 1st Session (1989). H.R. 1946, A Bill to…Authorize the Department of Veterans Affairs (VA) to Provide Home, Respite, and Dental Care. Washington: Government Printing Office, 1990. (GPO Microfiche no. 393, coordinate C13.)

2. U.S. House. 104th Congress, 1st Session (1995). "H.R. 3, A Bill to Control Crime." Version: 1; Version Date: 2/9/93. (Full Text of Bills: Congressional Universe Online Service. Bethesda, MD: Congressional Information Service.)

In the second illustration, the final element shows that the source is proprietary, or a commercial research service publication available to paying subscribers.

If you need more help on citing, consult these sources:

- Diane L. Garner and Diane H. Smith, *The complete guide to citing government information resources: a manual for writers and librarians* (rev. ed.) (Bethesda, MD: Congressional Information Service, 1993)
- Citing Government Information Sources Using MLA (Modern Language Association) Style at http://www.knowledgecenter.unr.edu/subjects/guides/government/cite.html
- Uncle Sam: Brief Guide to Citing Government Publications (University of Memphis Depository Library) at http://www.memphis.edu/govpub/citweb.php
- How Do I? Cite Publications Found in Databases for Thomas (Library of Congress) at http://www.memphis.edu/govpub/citweb.php

Remember to check your final product against the standard (Checklists, chapter 2).

# Three Examples

*Example 1. Legislative History of Nutritional Labeling 1906–1987*
*Overview*
Government has debated the topic of food labeling for nearly 100 years. Its history of legislation passed and court cases settled shows where we've come from and sets a precedent for future legislation. In 1906 Congress was concerned with establishing a basic standard for product labels to prevent consumers from being misled. Since then changes in science and public opinion have necessitated drafting new bills that fill gaps in legislation and place more restrictions on product labels to better protect and inform consumers. In the late 1980's that meant requiring nutritional labels on pre-packaged grids listing calories, fat, sugars, and other food values to inform an increasingly health-conscious America. Now in 2002, America's growing taste for increased portions of unhealthy fast food must be addressed by filling the gap in the Nutritional Labeling and Education Act exempting fast food from nutritional labels.

*Major Legislation and Legal Decisions*
*59th Congress*
H.R. *384: "The Food and Drug Act of 1906."* This act was the first on record in the United States that governed the contents of product labels. The legislature was concerned that manufacturers and distributors were labeling their products in a manner that misled consumers. Product labels that falsified ingredients or other product information were considered "adulterated" by the act. Through this legislation, food and drugs were required to be labeled with "distinctive names" that pertained directly to their contents and to have those names and the manufacturers' locations printed clearly. To enforce this bill, the Department of Agriculture was empowered to inspect, on demand, all packaged goods manufactured or transported within the United States, levying fines on violators.[1]

*76th Congress*
S.5: "The Federal Food, Drug and Cosmetic Act of 1938." This legislation was intended to replace the Food and Drug Act and cover a greater variety of products, including cosmetics, with more specific

language that clarified vagueness in the 1906 act. The new act regulated items on store shelves (an important addition), broadened the definition of "adulterated" to include spoiled or mishandled food, and placed tighter restrictions on how food could be labeled. If products claimed to serve specific dietary needs or produce certain health benefits, their labels had to contain a list of ingredients and be approved by the Secretary of Agriculture. The Secretary could now freely inspect not only the goods themselves, but also any factory, warehouse, or establishment that produced, stored, or sold them and freeze the sale of products that could be considered "adulterated." This was deemed much more effective than fines in deterring violators.[2]

### 85th Congress

H.R. 13254: "Food Additives Amendment." Created to amend the Federal Food, Drug and Cosmetic Act to cover food additives. This amendment shows government recognition of a growing trend in the food industry to use food additives and flavor enhancers with possible adverse health effects in order to lower costs. This amendment requires that before any food additive or flavor enhancer is used, its producers must disclose the additive's chemical composition and the results of a certified health study attesting to the additive's safety in the specific dosage. The effect was a dramatic decrease in the use of sodium and its derivatives as preserving agents.[3]

### 95th Congress

S.1750: "Saccharin Study and Labeling Act of 1977." This legislation is an extension of the Food Additives Amendment that called for the study of a possible link between saccharin consumption and cancer. At time of passage, saccharin, a sugar substitute, was a tremendously popular product and the implication that its usage could cause cancer was serious. The study found a conclusive link between saccharin usage and increased incidence of cancer in laboratory animals but it could not convince legislators there was a significant risk to humans. Instead of upsetting the marketplace based on "inconclusive" results, the Health, Labor, Education, and Pensions Committee implemented mandatory labeling. All products containing saccharin must clearly state: "Use of this product may be hazardous to your health. This product contains saccharin which has been determined to cause cancer in laboratory animals." What makes this bill noteworthy is that legislators approved of allowing an ingredient with alleged health risks to remain on the market provided that it had a clearly stated health advisory on the packaging.[4]

### 96th Congress
S.1196: "Disease Prevention and Health Promotion Act of 1978." The applicability of this legislation is its position on the effectiveness of disease prevention programs. The Committee on Health, Labor, Education, and Pensions found that contrary to popular opinion, "Americans are not fully informed about how to improve their own health and want more knowledge, that Federal, State and local governments have a role to play in providing that information, and that government at all levels has the capacity and the responsibility to help communities and individuals reduce the burden of illness through the prevention of disease and the promotion of good health."[5]

### 99th Congress
S.541: "Nutrition Information Labeling Act of 1985." A bill to amend the Federal Food, Drug and Cosmetic Act to require that a food's product label state the specific, common-name and the amount of each fat or oil contained in the food, the amount of saturated, polyunsaturated, and monounsaturated fats contained in the food, the amount of cholesterol contained in the food, and the amount of sodium and potassium contained in the food. This is the first bill to require nutritional labels, although it does not cover restaurants or raw agricultural products.

### 99th Congress
H.R. 6940: "Amend Food, Drug and Cosmetic Act." This bill requires baby formula to contain a prescribed nutritional content in order to be sold in the US. The significance is that government recognizes the need to not only disclose nutritional content but also regulate that content in order to ensure the well-being of the consumer.[7]

### Arbitration
In response to two petitions filed by The Center for Science in the Public Interest, New York State filed suit against McDonalds Corp.

alleging that their Chicken McNuggets were not the "pure chicken" advertised. In an out-of-court settlement McDonalds Corp. agreed to withdraw the ads and disclose the ingredients and nutritional content of their menu in pamphlets and posters at their New York restaurants. At the same time attorneys general in ten other states began the process of filing suit to require nutritional and ingredient disclosures from McDonalds and other major fast food chains. In a national settlement still in effect, McDonalds, Burger King, Jack in the Box, Kentucky Fried Chicken, and Wendy's agreed to offer separately printed nutritional information in pamphlets or on posters in stores around the country. This action resulted in McDonalds cutting back on beef-frying and discontinuing the use of yellow dye No. 5, which has been known to trigger allergies. However long-term compliance with the settlement has been inconsistent and only Jack in the Box has made information consistently available nationally. The rest of the chains only provided them in an average of 33 percent of locations.[8,9]

## 100th Congress
S.1325: "Fast Food Ingredient Information Act of 1987." This bill was written in response to a greater nutritional consciousness and the national settlement mentioned in the lawsuit above. The bill sought to amend the Food, Drug and Cosmetic Act to force fast food restaurants to label pre-packaged goods with nutritional labels and to display nutritional and ingredient information in clearly visible places in their restaurants. The bill also sought to amend the Federal Meat Inspection Act and the Poultry Products Inspection Act to allow for nutritional information to be posted in restaurants. President Reagan vetoed this bill because of possible, negative economic consequences.[10]

## 101st Congress
H.R. 3562: "The Nutrition Labeling and Education Act of 1989." An amendment to the Food, Drug and Cosmetic Act designed to expand on the requirements of the Nutritional Labeling and Education Act. The bill states that food will be deemed misbranded unless its label contains: serving size, number of servings, calories per serving and those derived from fat and saturated fat, and the amount of cholesterol,

sodium, total carbohydrates, sugars, total protein, and dietary fiber per serving or other unit. Authorizes the Secretary of Health and Human Services to require additional label information.[11]

### Sources

1. U.S. House of Representatives. 59th Congress. 2nd Session (1906). "H.R. 384 Food and Drug Act of 1906." Washington Government Printing Office, 1981.
2. U.S. Senate. 76th Congress. 1st Session (1938). "S.5 Federal Food, Drug and Cosmetic Act of 1938." Washington Government Printing Office, 1981.
3. U.S. House of Representatives. 85th Congress. 2nd Session (1958). "H.R. 13254 Food Additives Amendment." Washington Government Printing Office, 1981.
4. U.S. Senate. 95th Congress. 2nd Session (1977). "S.1750 Saccharin Study and Labeling Act of 1977." Washington Government Printing Office, 1978 (Thomas Bill Summary S.1750).
5. U.S. Senate. 96th Congress. 1st Session (1978). "S.1196 Disease Prevention and Health Promotion Act of 1978." Washington Government Printing Office, 1980 (Thomas Bill Summary S.1196).
6. U.S. Senate. 99th Congress. 1st Session (1985). "S.541 Nutrition Information Labeling Act of 1985." Washington Government Printing Office, 1985 (Thomas Bill Summary S.541).
7. U.S. House of Representatives. 99th Congress. 2nd Session (1986). "H.R. 6940 Amend Food, Drug and Cosmetic Act." Washington Government Printing Office, 1986 (Thomas Bill Summary H.R. 6940).
8. Clark, Charles S. "The Fast Food Shake-Up." *CQ Researcher,* November 8, 1991: 838–43.
9. *McDonalds to Introduce Nutrition Information Programs in New York: Press Release.* 30 April 1986. New York: New York State Attorney General's Office Consumer Protection Bureau.
10. U.S. Senate. 100th Congress. 1st Session (1987). "S.1325 Fast Food Ingredient Information Act of 1987." Washington Government Printing Office, 1987 (Thomas Bill Summary S.1325).

11. U.S. House of Representatives. 101st Congress. 1st Session (1989). "H.R. 3562 The Nutrition Labeling and Education Act of 1989." Washington Government Printing Office, 1989 (Thomas Bill Summary H.R. 3562).

---

**◄—◄ WHAT THIS EXAMPLE SHOWS.** This history of an issue includes litigation as well as multiple, selected legislative actions (Scope, this chapter). The author chose a report as the medium or presentation. It is titled, as a report typically is, rather than provided with a header, as a memo typically is. The title and overview connect this report to a context, a process underway in 2002 to amend existing legislation originated in 1989. This report traces landmark legislation leading up to the 1989 bill, the most recent action on the subject.

Organizationally, the report begins with an initial overview followed by summaries of major legislation arranged chronologically. Subheadings (congressional session and date) move an unfolding story of action along. Each summary concludes with a statement of the act's significance in a trend. The message of the report is to show that trend (Method, chapter 2). Thus, the concluding sentence of each summary reinforces the message by adding a new bit to the reader's recognition of the trend.

No purpose or audience for this report is identified; the undergraduate policy writing course assignment that prompted the research did not require it. That is a limitation on real world use, but this document nonetheless meets some of the expected standards for usability. It could serve a nonprofit organization wishing to inform its members about a current legislative priority.

Credibility is enhanced by the report's organization, which suggests care taken by an informed author to select key actions (well cited). Presentation here is authoritative and readable. The author has recognized a legislative trend and has selected, condensed, and ordered relevant legislation as well as litigation to highlight milestones in that trend. These choices and communication techniques encourage readers to agree with his position that new action is needed.

Careful citation here supports credibility. Readability is served by the way citations are handled. Citations are distributed across two locations in the text. Subheadings for summaries cite the legislative session, record number, and common name of each bill; a footnote at the end of each summary refers to citations at the end of the document, where the act is fully referenced using government record identifiers and bibliographic style (Task 3, this chapter; Checklists, chapter 2).

The document is designed for use. Despite its brevity, it could be more concise. Sentences are typically long and many sentences include unnecessary words (Checklists, chapter 2). The writer could shorten sentences to emphasize key information better, as illustrated here.

> **Original**. The bill sought to amend the Food, Drug and Cosmetic Act to force fast food restaurants to label prepackaged goods with nutritional labels and to display nutritional and ingredient information in clearly visible places in their restaurants. The bill also sought to amend the Federal Meat Inspection Act and the Poultry Products Inspection Act to allow for nutritional information to be posted in restaurants. (65 words)

> **Revised**.  The bill amends the Food, Drug and Cosmetic Act to require nutritional labeling of prepackaged goods and clearly visible display of ingredients by fast food restaurants. The Federal Meat Inspection Act and the Poultry Products Inspection Act are amended to allow ingredients display in restaurants. (45 words; 20 word reduction or 30 percent briefer)

---

The revision removes repetition of words ("bill sought to amend" and "nutritional information") and unnecessary explanation ("in clearly visible places").

### *Example 2. Legislative History of Banning the Use of Cell Phones While Driving*

*Memorandum*

> **To:**  North Carolina General Assembly Senator Dannelly; Representatives McAllister, Adams, B., Allen, Harrell, Hunter, Jones, Luebke, Michaux, Parmon, Tolson, and Womble.
>
> **From:**  AARP Steering Committee (simulated)
>
> **Date:**  April 7, 2008
>
> **Re:**  Ban on Cell Phones While Driving: A Legislative History

## Overview

Driver distractions lead each year to thousands of unnecessary and preventable deaths on our nation's streets and highways. One such distraction is the use of cell phones while driving. In his article analyzing legislative attempts to regulate cell phone use, Matthew Kalin cites studies that estimate "that six-hundred thousand collisions occur each year because of cellular phone use in vehicles" and that "ten to one-thousand deaths per year" occur as a result of cell phone use in vehicles (Kalin, 262, n 21). Other researchers have compared people talking on a cell phone while driving to drunk drivers. In a 2006 study of drivers in a driving simulator, professors at the University of Utah found that "people are as impaired when they drive and talk on a cell phone as they are when they drive intoxicated at the legal blood-alcohol limit of 0.08 percent" (Strayer, Drews & Crouch, 385–90). Lives can easily be saved by banning the use of cell phones while driving.

The North Carolina legislature has made a good start in this area. Current legislation protects our children from bus drivers distracted by their cell phones (N.C.G.S. §20–140.6) and inexperienced drivers are not allowed to use a cell phone while driving (N.C.G.S. §20–137.3). Unfortunately, your bills to amend Chapter 20 of the North Carolina General Statutes to ban the use of cell phones by all drivers have not yet been passed into law.

The following review of current legislation shows that the important work of making our streets and highways safer from the dangers posed by distracted drivers has begun. Unfortunately, current legislation falls dangerously short in the area of cell phone use by drivers. For now, current legislation only forbids a fraction of the millions of people driving while using their cell phones. Consequently, we can expect innocent motorists and pedestrians to continue to be injured and killed on our roads and highways by drivers too caught up with their telephone conversations to pay attention to their surroundings. Now is the time to resume your call to protect everyone on our roads and highways from the danger posed by drivers distracted by cell phone use. North Carolina can become a leader in protecting motorists from the deadly consequences of drivers distracted by their cell phones by banning the use of cell phones by all drivers.

*Major Legislation–North Carolina*

General Assembly of North Carolina, 2005 Session

**Senate Bill 1289 (Third Edition): "Cell Phone Use by Drivers Under 18 Prohibited" (G.S. 20–137.3).** This Bill makes it illegal for drivers between the ages of 15 and 18 years of age to use a cell phone while driving. Specifically, this bill

- Makes the use of a cell phone by a person between the ages of 15 and 18 years of age while driving an infraction
- Provides for a fine of $25 (but does not assess court costs or result in points against the driver's license or insurance)
- Further punishes a teenage driver by not allowing the driver to advance to the next level of licensure for an additional 6 months
- Includes a ban on the use of hands-free phones, Internet gaming devices, electronic music devices, and the like.

General Assembly of North Carolina, 2007 Session

**House Bill 183 (Third Edition): "Ban Cell Phone Use by School Bus Drivers" (G.S. 20–140.6).** This Bill created Section 20–140.6 of the North Carolina General Statutes, making it illegal to "engage in a call on a mobile phone or use a digital media device while operating a public or private school bus" (N.C.G.S. §20–140.6). Specifically, this bill

- Makes the use of a cell phone by a bus driver a Class 2 misdemeanor
- Provides for a punishment of up to 60 days and a fine of no less than $100
- Allows for emergency exceptions

While the above protections are an important start, the AARP agrees with you that more is required. We applaud the following two bills that all of you worked so diligently on and hope you will continue your good work and see them passed into law. In fact, we encourage you to go even further in the name of safety—consider banning all cell telephone use (with the current exceptions), *including* hands-free phones.

**Senate Bill 1399: "Ban Mobile Phone Use While Driving."** This bill was re-referred to the Committee on Judiciary II (Criminal) on May 24, 2007. If passed, it would ban the use of cell phones while driving, but allow drivers to use hands-free phones while driving. It also allows for emergency exceptions and use by police, firefighters, and ambulance drivers. The use of a cell phone would be an infraction, with a penalty of a fine of $25.00. There would be no point assessment to the driver's North Carolina driver's license nor any insurance surcharge assessed as a result of a violation of this section. Also, this infraction would "not constitute negligence per se or contributory negligence by the driver in any action for the recovery of damages arising out of the operation, ownership, or maintenance of a motor vehicle."

**House Bill 1104: "Ban Cell Phone Use While Driving."** This bill was re-referred to the Committee on Judiciary III on May 18, 2005. If passed, it would ban the use of cell phones while driving, but allow drivers to use hands-free phones while driving. It also allows for emergency exceptions and use by police, firefighters, and ambulance drivers. The use of a cell phone while driving would be an infraction, with a penalty of a $100.00 fine and costs of court. No points would be assessed to the driver's North Carolina driver's license as a result of this infraction.

*Legislation in Other Jurisdictions*
According to a 2004 review of traffic safety legislation, eighteen states and the District of Columbia have passed laws regarding the use of cell phones while driving (Savage, Sundeen and Mejeur, 2004). Here is a sample of the legislation currently in effect in other states:

California: Section 23103 of the California Vehicle Code makes it illegal to operate a handheld device while driving, and the fine is $20.00 for the first offense and $50.00 for each offense thereafter (Barmby, 345).

New York: Section 1225 of the New York code bans the use of hand-held cell phones while driving, and a violation of same is considered an infraction, punishable by a fine of not more than $100.00 (New York Consolidated Law Service).

New Jersey: Section 39:4–97.3 of the New Jersey Statutes makes it illegal to use a cell phone while driving unless it is a "hands-free wireless telephone." A driver in New Jersey can be cited for such a violation only if she is detained for another driving or criminal violation at the same time. A person who violates this law is to be fined "no less than $100 or more than $250" and no points are assessed to the driver's license or insurance (LexisNexis New Jersey Annotated Statutes).

In addition to state legislation, a number of towns and cities implemented their own bans on the use of cell phones while driving. Brooklyn, Ohio was the first municipality in the U.S. to ban cellular phone use while driving, and Hilltown, Pennsylvania, also banned the use of cell phones while driving (Kalin, 244). Fort Campbell military base in Kentucky banned hand-held cellular phone use while driving (Kalin, 245). However, as you know, municipality ordinances can be overruled by a state law, "preemption," if the state legislators think it appropriate.

Again, we hope North Carolina can become a leader in providing for safer streets and highways by banning both hand-held *and hands-free* cell phone use while driving.

*Federal Response*
On July 18, 2000, Congress began hearings to discuss possible legislative solutions (Cripps, 107). The House of Representatives introduced the Driver Distraction Prevention Act of 2000, a study implemented to explore the impact of driver distractions on highway safety (Cripps, 107). However, to date, Congress has not implemented a policy to protect drivers from the hazards posed by drivers distracted by cell phone use.

## Works Cited

Barmby, Erin. "Review of selected 2007 California legislation: Vehicle: Chapter 290: California's message to hang up and pay attention." *McGeorge Law Review* 38 (2007): 42–52.

Cripps, Jr., Jesse. "Dialing while driving: The battle over cell phone use on America's roadways." *Gonzaga Law Review* 37 (2001/2002): 89–119.

House Bill 183. "Ban cell phone use while driving." Online: North Carolina General Assembly homepage 9 April 2008. http://www.ncleg.net/gascripts/BillLookUp/BillLookUp.pl?Session=2005&BillID=H1104

Kalin, Matthew. "The 411 on cellular phone use: An analysis of the legislative attempts to regulate cellular phone use by drivers." *Suffolk University Law Review* 39 (January 2005): 233–262. Citing, Hahn, Robert & Patrick M. Dudley. "The disconnect between law and policy analysis: A case study of drivers and cell phones, *Administrative Law Review* 55 (2003): 127, 130.

New Jersey Statutes Annotated 39:4–97.3 (2004). Online: LexisNexis (TM) New Jersey Annotated Statutes 8 April 2008. http://www.lexisnexis.com/us [Subscription required] New York Vehicle & Traffic Law 1225-c (2001). Online: New York Consolidated Law Service, Matthew Bender & Company, Inc. 8 April 2008. http://www.lexisnexis.com/us/ [Subscription required]

Savage, Melissa, Sundeen, Matt, and Mejeur, Jeanne, "Traffic safety and public health: State legislative Action, 2004." National Conference of State Legislators' Transportation Series, (December 2004, No. 20). [Purchase required]. Online, 8 April 2008. http://www.ncsl.org/print/transportation/04trafficsafety.pdf

Senate Bill 1399. "Ban mobile phone use while driving." Online: North Carolina General Assembly homepage. 9 April 2008. http://www.ncleg.net/gascripts/BillLookUp/BillLookUp.pl?BillID=S1399&Session=2007

Strayer, David, Frank Drews & Dennis Crouch. "A comparison of the cell phone driver and the drunk driver." *Human Factors* 48 (Summer 2006): 381–391.

Stutts, Jane, Donald Reinfurt, Loren Staplin & Eric Rodgman. "The role of driver distraction in traffic crashes." AAA Foundation for Traffic Safety Report. (May 2001): 1–63. [Purchase required]. Online: 9 April 2008. http://www.aaafoundation.org/pdf/distraction.pdf

## Example 3. Legislative History of the Earned Income Tax Credit

This legislative history is incorporated in a policy brief advocating reform of the Earned Income Tax Credit (EITC). Other sections of the brief shown elsewhere in this guide: policy analysis and proposals (Example 3, chapter 4) and summary of findings (Example, chapter 6).

### Policy Significance and Context: The EITC and Tax Policy

As currently structured, the EITC provides a tax credit for low-income households that is based on income and family status and is fully refundable.

...

The original political debates in the early 1970s over the EITC reflected some differences over its primary purpose: whether to provide payroll tax relief to all low-wage workers or to increase the labor force participation of less-skilled workers who might otherwise rely on public assistance benefits to support their families, or both. Ultimately, Congress structured the tax credit to do both, but only for families with children, thus placing more emphasis on its policy role in welfare reform. In this way, the EITC fulfilled its original tenets as set forth by Congress: "an added bonus or incentive for low-income people to work," and as a way to reduce welfare dependency by "inducing individuals with families receiving federal assistance to support themselves" (U.S. Congress, Senate, 1975).

The earliest proposals for an earned income credit emerged in response to ongoing debates about a minimum income for all Americans and increasing concerns about the impact of rising payroll taxes on low-income workers... Traditional forms of individual income tax relief, either by reducing positive tax rates or raising personal exemptions, were of more limited assistance to those low-income workers and their families whose federal income tax liability was already zero. Policymakers began to explore whether federal income tax relief should be delivered only as an "exemption," a "deduction"—which would reduce the amount of *earned* income subject to tax—or as a tax credit that directly offsets tax payments or liability. Some elected officials viewed such tax assistance as part of a broader program to provide a basic social safety net and reduce or eliminate poverty—as well as a convenient administrative way to deliver cash benefits to low-income families. Others viewed this individual tax benefit more broadly as a way to offset the burdens of other taxes that all low and moderate-wage workers pay, regardless of family status, such as payroll taxes, excise taxes, state and local sales, property, and income taxes.

Under existing federal tax law in 1974, workers were not required to pay income taxes unless their incomes exceeded the amount of the minimum standard deduction plus the sum of available personal exemptions. The House Ways and Means Committee concluded in its 1975 report accompanying legislation creating the EITC: "If the problems of low-wage workers are the regressive effects of payroll taxes then the credit should be available to all low-income individuals, regardless of marital status or children" (U.S. Congress, House, 1975). The House version of the EITC covered 28 million taxpayers. In order to keep costs down, the House reduced the proposed tax credit from 10 percent to 5 percent. The one-year revenue loss was projected to be $2.9 billion, all of which would be received by workers whose incomes were below $6,000.

Whereas the House version depicted the EITC as payroll tax relief, the Senate Finance Committee's bill depicted the EITC as welfare reform. While the Senate adopted the general concept of the earned income credit, it revised it to improve "its impact on the low-income taxpayers with children" (U.S. Congress, Senate, 1975). Since many low-wage workers were from non-poor families, extending earning subsidies to all workers could be "expensive and inefficient in reaching the poor," and thus, the Senate plan restricted its subsidy to families with children and applied the subsidy to total family earnings. (U.S. Congress, Senate, 1975). This change involved a revenue loss of $1.5 billion, or about one-half of the House proposal (U.S. Congress, Senate, 1975). Congress, in the end, accepted the Senate position that the "most significant objective of the EITC should be to assist in encouraging people to obtain employment, reducing the unemployment rate and reducing the welfare rolls; more importantly, most federal welfare programs apply to married couples with dependent children and it is in this area that the EITC can be most effective in reducing any tax disincentive to work" (U.S. Congress, Senate, 1975). By limiting the credit only to low-income workers with families, Congress reduced the number of potential "beneficiaries" from 28 million to 6.4 million. When the tax credit was enacted in 1975, it generated little attention. The initial credit amount was equal to only 10 percent of total income up to $4,000 (providing a maximum benefit of $400) and then it phased out at 10 percent until income reached $8,000...

The EITC continued to be offered to eligible workers for the next several years and was made a permanent piece of the Internal Revenue Code (IRC) in 1978. Since that time, it has undergone significant expansions with broad bipartisan support. The credit was expanded in 1986 under President Ronald Reagan, in 1990 under President George H.W. Bush, and again in 1993 under President Bill Clinton when the size of the credit was doubled and a small credit was added for workers without children....EITC expansions also were used to off-set the regressive effects of increases in payroll taxes and in gasoline, alcohol, and tobacco excise taxes for families with children. The 1986 Tax Reform Act explicitly cited this principle of eliminating income tax burdens for families with incomes near the poverty level as the reason for increasing the dollar amounts of standard deductions and personal exemptions. The Omnibus Budget Reconciliation Acts of 1990 and 1993 (OBRA-90 and OBRA-93) increased the credit rate, introduced a larger EITC (with a higher credit rate and more earnings eligible for the matching credit) for families with two or more children, and intro-duced a small EITC for childless workers. Each of these increases was phased-in over three years. Consequently, the credit rates increased every year from 1990 to 1995.

...

## The Rise of an EITC for Single Workers

In 1993, President Clinton urged making the EITC available to very low-income workers who did not have children; opponents warned that it would be difficult to broaden the EITC to wage earners without children "without breaking the bank."...As part of the final legislative agreement in 1993, the EITC was extended for the first time to work-ers without children. In addition to offsetting a portion of these various tax increases, the establishment of the EITC for poor childless work-ers partially addressed a piece of unfinished business from the 1986 Tax Reform Act....One of those goals, often espoused by President Reagan, was to eliminate federal income taxes on workers below the poverty line so they would not be taxed deeper into poverty.... The EITC raised the income level at which these workers would begin to owe income tax, but that level still remains below the poverty line.

After the 1994 elections, Republicans proposed several new limits on eligibility to the EITC....House and Senate proposals erased some of the expansion in the credit achieved by President Clinton as part of his 1993 budget plan....Under the 2001 tax reforms, President Bush allowed more married couples to become eligible for the earned-income tax credit....The president also proposed a permanent extension of EITC-related provisions enacted in 2001 as part of his 10-year tax cut bill.

Some reformers charge that one of the biggest challenges is the fact that the United States has become divided between a growing class of people who pay no federal income taxes and a shrinking class of people who are bearing the lion's share of the tax burden.

...

Not coincidentally, the latest round of tax cuts follows on the Council of Economic Advisers' (CEA) Economic Report to the President, released in February 2003, which made the case that low-to-moderate income families do not shoulder a fair share of the income tax burden. The document lays the intellectual groundwork for policies that would greatly simplify the tax system, but that would arguably raise the federal tax burden on lower-income workers, while reducing that on the affluent....In keeping with this, Treasury Department economists are drafting new ways to calculate the distribution of tax burdens among different income classes, and those results are expected to highlight what Bush Administration officials view as a rising tax burden on the rich and a declining burden on the poor...

As part of the President George W. Bush's Advisory Panel on Federal Tax Reform, several proposals were advanced to address the needs of low-wage workers. Robert Greenstein, executive director of the Center on Budget and Policy Priorities, focused specifically on the role of the Earned Income Tax Credit in improving tax fairness when single workers begin owing income tax several hundred dollars *below* the poverty line...

...

## What Role for the States?

In the absence of federal reform, states have experimented with EITC reforms. As of January 2006, 18 states and the District of Columbia have adopted Earned Income Tax Credits. Most recently, Delaware and Virginia enacted new EITCs, Illinois and Oregon changed their state EITC from non-refundable to refundable, and several states and the District of Columbia, expanded existing EITCs. In addition, three local governments—Montgomery County, Md., New York City, and San Francisco—offer local EITCs.

...

(The policy brief can be found at http://www.law.unc.edu/documents/ poverty/publications/gittermanpolicybrief.pdf. Also see Gitterman 2003 and Gitterman, et al. 2008.)

---

**WHAT THESE EXAMPLES SHOW** These examples illustrate records research for advocacy and analysis purposes. Example 2 is an issue history; Example 3 is a single law history. They exemplify the two main motivations for writing legislative histories, either to chronicle actions on an issue across jurisdictions (Example 2) or to characterize a pattern of legislative intent for a particular law over time (Example 3).

In Example 2 an attorney representing a nonprofit organization (simulated) conducts records research to put the organization's advocacy into a context of precedents. In Example 3 policy analysts search the records of prior reform to support their recommendation of new reform.

The examples differ as documentation (Viewpoint 3, chapter 2). Both exhibit knowledge that is expected in a legislative history. However, they communicate in different forms, illustrating the variety of functions that legislative history serves. Example 2 is a report in memorandum form. An attorney or a librarian or an organization staff member might prepare such reports for a user's particular interest or purpose. Research would have the limited objective of developing that user's knowledge. Example 3 has a broader objective. In Example 3 the legislative and administrative record is interpreted, not only reported. The interpretation shows the direction, including changes of direction, of governmental action over time. Individual policy actions are recontextualized in a pattern of intent. This interpretive history is used as evidence supporting a recommendation. Thus, in Example 3, interpretive legislative history functions rhetorically to persuade. It says that the recommended action fits within precedent and is possibly achievable.

Both Example 2 and 3 are written for silent reading, not speaking. Sentence structure and length are indications. In example 3 sentences, while long, are constructed understandably. In Example 2, however, excess words in many sentences strain a reader's attention. Readability would be improved by removing unnecessary repetition that causes wordiness in sentences, and by varying sentence length. In the following instance, repetition is italicized in the original. The revision has reduced repetition, shortened phrases, and varied sentence length.

> **Original.** *Unfortunately*, your bills to amend Chapter 20 of the North Carolina General Statutes to ban the *use of cell phones by all drivers* have not yet been passed into law. The following review of *current legislation* shows that the important work of making our streets and highways safer from dangers posed by distracted drivers has begun. *Unfortunately, current legislation* falls dangerously short in the area of *cell phone use by drivers.* (71 words)

> **Revised.** Unfortunately, your amendments to Chapter 20 of the North Carolina General Statutes to ban the use of cell phones by all drivers are not yet law The following review of current legislation shows that the important work of reducing risk posed by distracted drivers has begun. But it falls dangerously short. (51 words)

## Summary and Preview

To ask persuasively for government action, you must know what government has done, has not done, or has intended in regard to your concern. Legislative records research develops your knowledge of prior action. Chapter 6, next, prepares you to use your knowledge of the record in making policy arguments.

## References

Garner, D. L., and D. H. Smith. 1993. *The complete guide to citing government information resources: A manual for writers and librarians.* Rev. ed. Bethesda, MD: Congressional Information Service.

Gitterman, Daniel P. 2003. Tax credits for working families. http://www. brookings.edu/reports/2003/08childrenfamilies_gitterman.aspx

Gitterman, Daniel P., Lucy S. Gorham, and Jessica L. Dorrance. 2008. Expanding the EITC for single workers and couples without children: Tax relief for all low-wage workers. *Georgetown Journal on Poverty Law and Policy*: 15, 2, 245–84.

# CHAPTER 6

# Position Paper: Know the Arguments

## Key Concept

- policy argumentation

Making public policy requires making arguments and understanding arguments. This chapter helps you to argue a position, to critically analyze your own and other arguments, and to recognize grounds for cooperation as well as competition among arguments.

A policy argument supports a claim that something should or should not be done. Such arguments have two main components: a claim and its support. The claim asserts what should or should not be done. Or it takes a position on a debated question. Support for the claim presents the evidence, interpretations, and assumptions that lead to making that claim. The argument's presentation should be intentionally constructed to convince others to accept the claim and to agree with the position.

Arguments are made both implicitly and explicitly. Implicit arguments are unstated elements of problem definitions. For example, to define cell phone use while driving as a public safety risk is to argue implicitly that government has a role in regulating drivers' risky behaviors. Implicit arguments are usually not intended to deceive. They are simply the unacknowledged structures of thought within a position. Position takers should be critically aware of their implicit arguments as well as their explicit arguments. They should critically analyze other positions for implicit as well as explicit arguments, too.

Why argue? In policy work, you argue to disclose what you think and what you want to accomplish. You do not argue to prove or disprove; you do not argue only for or against. The popular notion of argument as a quarrel between adversaries distorts argument's function and significance for policy purposes. Similarly, the legal notion of argument as contestation by opposing parties is inadequate. In policy making, there are always more than two interested parties. In democratic process, you engage ideas, not adversaries. You argue to add your position to the debate and to the possibilities.

To illustrate, an undergraduate student government representative wants to change the culture at her university to discourage drug and alcohol abuse. As a dormitory resident advisor, she knows first hand that campus culture encourages recreational drug use and underage as well as binge drinking. Initially, she took the position that punitive action was called for. As a member of the Judicial Affairs subcommittee of the student assembly, she had accomplished revisions in the university judicial system to increase sanctions against drug and alcohol use as well as penalties for violations. However, the sanctions and penalties had little impact on the character of campus life. Consequently, her position has changed. In a report that she authors for the student assembly's Judicial Affairs subcommittee addressed to the Dean of Student Affairs, she now argues that judicial action is not enough. She cites evidence from dormitory life based on her resident advising experience. She claims that comprehensive action is needed to reduce dependence on drugs and alcohol for social interaction. She specifies needs to update university policy, to reorganize administration of campus life, and to design educational interventions. In her choice of proposed solutions, she has anticipated opposing arguments by other student government leaders and by some university administrators favoring either the status quo or increased sanctions and enforcement. Her purpose for arguing is to deepen the campus debate on drugs and alcohol by focusing on the central question of why campus life encourages their use.

At the same university, another undergraduate majoring in public policy studies serves as an officer of a national student association that advocates drug policy reform. In that role, she writes a policy memo to the director of a national drug control policy institute stating her association's position on recent legislation and asking the director to rethink the institute's support for recent amendments to the Higher Education Act (HEA) of 1965. (Proposals to amend typically refer to the original legislation being amended. Major acts such as the 1965 HEA are amended, often, over many years.) Those amendments barred students with drug-related convictions from receiving federal financial aid for education unless they undergo rehabilitation. The student leader presents the association's opposition to the amendments on two grounds, fairness and feasibility. On fairness, she argues that reducing eligibility for aid to higher education hurts working class families and discriminates against people of color. Regarding the discriminatory effects, she elaborates with empirical evidence showing that 95 percent of imprisoned drug offenders in New York State are people of color while the majority of drug users are not. She interprets this evidence as showing racial bias in drug law enforcement at the state level. On feasibility, she argues that the amendments cannot be implemented because they do not call for allocation of funds to pay for rehabilitation. She anticipates rebuttals by the director of the drug control policy institute but she does not respond to them in the policy memo. Its purpose is to represent the student association's perspective on a current drug policy reform proposal.

What does policy argument do? It displays the reasoning that underlies positions. In collective public deliberation, arguments disclose the universe of definitions of the problem. In practical politics, argument reveals commonalities and conflicts. These are the grounds on which a course of action can be deliberated. Commonalities among arguments can point to potential cooperation, perhaps compromise, cosponsorship, or coalition forming. Conflicts give insight into competing interests and values that must be taken into account in negotiating a solution.

In another illustration, a farmer has applied to local government for a permit to operate a large-scale industrial farm called a confined animal feeding operation (CAFO). In the rural municipality where the farmer lives, the zoning ordinance allows such operations only as a "conditional" use of land zoned for agricultural uses. "Conditional" uses require case-by-case decisions by local officials on whether to permit or not permit the use. The decision process includes a public hearing inviting residents and others to comment on the proposed use. In the hearing held on the farmer's application, arguments including the following are made:

- farmers have rights to use and to benefit from their property; to deny this permit is to violate the farmer's private property rights

- nearby homeowners have rights to use and to benefit from their property; to grant this permit is to violate the neighbors' private property rights

- large-scale confined animal farming pollutes the environment and creates human health risks; to grant this permit is to fail to protect natural resources and the public welfare

- large-scale confined animal farming is regulated and better monitored for compliance with antipollution control than unregulated small-scale farming; to grant this permit will not harm local water or community health

- farming is an endangered occupation; to grant this permit will enable a local family-owned farm to succeed by expanding operations and will help to preserve farming in the region

- farming is an endangered occupation, and industrial farming is driving smaller farmers out of business; to grant this permit is to harm the local economy, which is still based on diverse types of farming

If you were a local official, how would you decide this request? Clearly, many arguable issues and competing positions are involved. You might permit or not permit the use, basing your decision either way on a single argument. Alternatively, you might focus on a commonality among the arguments, such as the wish to preserve rights or the wish to protect public health. Then you might ask the farmer and the neighbors to work out a compromise application. You might delay your decision until you have a revised application that takes specified risks to the community into account.

Argument has its limits in practical policy work, of course. "Arguments are made by all players all the time; as a result they have limited effectiveness. Although arguments are a necessary ingredient to any strategy, they never work by themselves" (Coplin and O'Leary 1998, p.107). As the local government illustration suggests, you might need to craft a political compromise along with arguing your position. Also, you must recognize political conditions that will determine your argument's effectiveness. How well an argument is received has more to do with majority control in a governing body than with the quality of the argument. In the local government illustration, the official who represents majority political power might have sufficient influence to force a compromise. The minority power representative might not, unless others can be persuaded to join the minority's position.

When is argument important? Argument can make a difference at several points in the process. Arguments matter before a policy process begins, as positions are being developed. They matter at the outset of a process, as stakes are declared and agendas set. They matter again at the end of the process, when a decision is being made.

## How to Argue in a Position Paper

*Goal*: Critical awareness of your own position, critical understanding of other positions, and willingness to consider and to engage other positions.

*Objective*: Reasoned argument for a position showing awareness of alternative positions and reasoning.

*Product*: Written document that explicitly argues and aims to persuade. A genre commonly used by policy analysts outside government is the position paper (sometimes called a discussion paper, "white" paper, or policy brief). Products might run to book-length in some circumstances, or they might be much shorter, perhaps two to six pages.

*Scope*: Either a "big picture" of conditions, causes, or consequences relating to a problem or a "little picture" of significant particulars.

*Strategy*: To know your position in relation to others. To consider your position ethically and politically:

- make a list of the known positions on the problem
- ask and answer the questions "What does my position have in common with others on this list?" and "How does my position differ from or conflict with others on the list?"

- note specific commonalities, differences, and conflicts of values, assumptions, or ideas between your position and other positions
- identify potential grounds for cooperation and for competition

## Task #1. Outline your Argument

If you are authoring a position paper for a professional association or for a nonprofit organization, make sure you understand its mission and how the position you are taking relates to the mission. Be clear on that relationship. Consult before deviating from the mission.

In most cases, you can use the following outline for informal arguments to construct the logic of a policy position:

- problem
- issue
- question about the issue that has at least two answers and is therefore arguable
- claim (the arguer's assertion or answer to the question)
- support:
  - justification
    - reasons ("because" or the relevance of the assertion)
    - assumptions ("basis" or the values, beliefs, principles, and licenses that motivate the assertion as well as the authority represented in the assertion)
  - elaboration
    - grounds (supporting evidence for the reasons and the assumptions)
    - limits (constraints the arguer would place on the claim)
  - anticipated reactions (potential responses from others holding diverse positions)
    - cooperative or supporting assertions
    - competitive or opposing assertions
    - altogether different assumptions
    - challenges to reasons or to grounds

The outline does not include rebuttal. A position paper should not rebut. Rather, its reasoning should exhibit anticipation of reactions.

## Task #2. Write the Position Paper

Review the Method in chapter 2 before you write to get the rhetorical framework for your document in mind.

By consciously thinking about your position in relation to others
(*Strategy*, above) and outlining the logic of your argument (Task 1,
above), you have already begun to plan the contents of the document. That does not mean that the document's contents should
simply fill in the outline, however. Think of the outline as a skel-
eton. The contents are its body, clothed for a particular occasion.
Content might vary on different occasions while the argument
stays the same.

The message that the document conveys will be your claim or
your answer to the issue question. When arguing in a policy context,
you must be aware of your authority for making a claim. Authority in
argument has two meanings, a practical meaning and a conceptual
meaning. In practical politics, authority means credibility and power.
Credibility derives more from a role than from a credential such as
specialized expertise, although that might be relevant. (The phrase
"consider the source" evokes this meaning of authority.) Any role
carries its own kind of power, whether it's the power of elected or
appointed office or the power of citizenship or community member-
ship. Conceptually, authority means persuasiveness. Authority in
this sense is a function of evidence and analysis. Authoritative writing convinces by the quality of its support for claims and its care for
using information reliably. (The phrase "you can rely on it" evokes
this meaning of authority.) At their best, authoritative arguments
are both credible and persuasive.

The document must clearly show whose position it communicates. Yours? That of an organization that you represent?

You must anticipate reactions to your position. Go back to the
list you made of positions alternative to your own (see *Strategy*,
above). For each position on the list, note the reaction you might
accordingly expect, and then rank the reactions in order of importance to you. Anticipate responses, but do not rebut them in the
position paper (unless you are directed to do so). Keep the focus
on your position.

Condense greatly, for now. You will likely have later opportunity
to elaborate. However, keep this in mind: it will cost you credibility
to ignore information your readers might deem important in light
of other arguments. Possibly put detailed evidence in an appendix.
Charts, tables, other graphics, or extended textual materials, should
normally be appended. However, the choice to append important

details should rest on knowing the circumstances in which the position paper will be read and used. Writers especially should know whether all readers will see the entire document, including appendices. Use a standard citation style for identifying sources. Modern Language Association (MLA) style or American Psychological Association (APA) style might be sufficient. Or legal citation style might be needed.

If you are authoring a position paper that speaks for a group or organization, plan to allow adequate time for consultation. Are you the sole author, or do you have collaborators? Are you ghostwriting for someone else? Plan also to allow for review and revision, possibly multiple reviews calling for multiple revisions. Who will review drafts? Who will make revisions? Remember to check the final draft against expected standards (Checklists, chapter 2). Revise further, if needed, before releasing.

## *Example*

The policy brief sampled here exhibits multiple communication subgenres within a single, lengthy (55-page) document. They are policy analysis, legislative history, critical analysis of policy discourse, and argumentation. Here, argumentation is shown. Other subgenres are shown elsewhere (Example 3, chapter 4; Example 3, chapter 5).

To illustrate argumentation, the brief's abstract, introduction, summary of findings, and overview of policy options are sampled next here. Immediately following, an outline applies the logical organization suggested in Task 1 to show this argument's structure. The outline refers to the entire brief, not only to the parts sampled in this chapter. To recognize the argument's development and coherence throughout the original document, you must read the entire document in reference to the outline. There are two ways of reading it here, either outline-first or brief-first. You might first read the outline and the sample in this chapter followed by Example 3, chapter 4 and Example 3, chapter 5, referring back to the outline here as needed. Alternatively, first read the full brief (using access information provided at the end of the sample here), then read the outline here, referring back to the brief as needed. Either way, your objective is to "toggle" between the outline and the brief, in order to discern the logical structure of argument in an extensive written document.

### Expanding the EITC for Single Workers and Couples With*out* Children (aka tax relief for low-wage workers)

Daniel P. Gitterman, Lucy S. Gorham, Jessica L. Dorrance

A Policy Brief prepared for the Center on Poverty, Work and Opportunity at the University of North Carolina at Chapel Hill
January 2007

## Abstract

The Earned Income Tax Credit (EITC), the nation's largest anti-poverty program, now provides tax benefits of roughly $39 billion dollars a year to over 21 million households. By supplementing the earnings of low-wage workers, the EITC "makes work pay." The EITC's popularity can be attributed to its providing both work incentives and tax relief. In 1993, Congress extended a small earned income credit to singles and childless couples; however, about 96 percent of EITC dollars still go to families with children. This discussion paper argues that, while the emphasis of the EITC on rewarding work for families with children deserves continued primacy, expansion of the EITC to childless single workers and married couples without children deserves greater attention for the following reasons:

- The disproportionate and growing income tax burden (payroll, sales, excise) faced by this group of workers;
- The growing segment of workers at the bottom of the labor market, particularly single men with low levels of education and training, who remain confined to low-wage jobs;
- The strict separation in our thinking between households with and without children requires reexamination, given the growing number of children with non-custodial parents; and,
- With a national savings rate below zero, the need to facilitate asset building for all low-wage workers, including those without children.

We recommend expanding the EITC for single workers and childless married couples with a range of policy recommendations, each targeting specific new subgroups of EITC recipients and addressing a slightly different purpose:

- Increase the EITC from 7.65 percent to 15.3 percent of earnings up to $8,080 in order to directly offset payroll taxes; and adjust the phase-in and phase-out ranges;
- Lower the age requirement for single and childless workers to qualify for the EITC from 25 to 21 to target greater workforce participation incentives to young workers just entering the labor market and making major decisions about work;

- Encourage single low-income workers to claim the Advance (monthly) EITC and use the increase in employee payroll earnings to contribute toward health care insurance premiums; and,
- Link the EITC to asset building options such as matched savings accounts for education and training, homeownership, retirement, and entrepreneurship. In addition, remove asset limits for other public benefit programs, particularly to assist those with disabilities to enter the labor market and build assets.

### Introduction

The Earned Income Tax Credit (EITC) is a refundable federal income tax credit first enacted with bipartisan political support in 1975. The EITC encourages low-income workers with children to enter and remain in the labor market by supplementing the earnings of those working for low wages, thus "making work pay."...In this policy brief, we explore three questions:

1. What do existing policy research and current data tell us about whether the original two goals of the EITC—payroll tax relief and encouraging employment—are being met adequately for the sub-groups of childless single and married workers;
2. Are there additional rationales that would justify an expansion of the EITC for this sub-group; and,
3. What policy changes could accomplish all or some of these policy goals?

...

### Summary of Key Findings

...

This brief argues that, while the salient effects of the EITC on reducing child poverty and rewarding work for low-income workers with children deserve continued primacy, the potential for providing needed economic support and greater federal tax relief to childless single and married workers deserves immediate attention for the following reasons:

- The disproportionate tax burden faced by low-wage single workers, which has worsened since the EITC was enacted in

1975, make tax relief an even greater priority as an issue of tax fairness.... If any workers need a tax cut, we argue that these workers do.

• A growing segment of workers at the bottom of the labor market... remain confined to low-wage jobs.... Leaving this group at the margins of the labor market undermines the strength of the workforce, communities, and families.

*Policy Options for an Expansion of the EITC for Childless Workers...*
Politically, at both the federal and state level, an expanded EITC could embody both progressive and conservative values by: (1) rewarding those who work with an earnings subsidy; (2) providing the greatest benefits to those with the greatest need; (3) offsetting the tax burden on working poor singles and childless married couples struggling to make ends meet; (4) providing incentives for people to enter the workforce who otherwise might not do so; (5) achieving these ends without increasing employer costs, without creating hiring disincentives and with minimal government bureaucracy; and (6) helping single workers and families without children, and potentially many more, to build assets for homeownership, education, and retirement when combined with other institutional supports such as matched savings programs....

(The full document including, tables, charts, citations and references can be found at http://www.law.unc.edu/documents/poverty/publications/gittermanpolicybrief.pdf. Also see Gitterman 2003 and Gitterman, et al. 2008.)

————

➤ **WHAT THIS EXAMPLE SHOWS.** Thinking that the legislator who requested this brief might run for president, the authors used the policy brief as an opportunity to focus the potential candidate's attention on the small tax credit available to workers without children. Because the EITC had become a major instrument of antipoverty policy, the authors argued to extend some of its benefits. The brief illustrates authoritative argument. The outline presented next shows its structure.

*Outline of the argument to expand the Earned Income Tax Credit (EITC) in the United States*

*Problem*: EITC eligibility limited to families with children.
*Issue*: Ineligibility of single workers and couples without children.
*Question*: Should EITC cover single workers and couples without children?
*Claim*: The EITC should be expanded to childless single workers and married couples without children for multiple reasons.
*Support*: Justification, elaboration, and limits.

- justification
  - reasons
    - the disproportionate and growing income tax burden (payroll, sales, excise) faced by this group of workers
    - the growing segment of workers at the bottom of the labor market, particularly single men with low levels of education and training, who remain confined to low-wage jobs
    - the strict separation in our thinking between households with and without children requires reexamination, given the growing number of children with noncustodial parents
    - with a national savings rate below zero, the need to facilitate asset building for all low-wage workers, including those without children
  - assumptions
    - original policy goals of the EITC are to provide work incentives and tax relief for low-wage workers
    - the present tax code is unfair to low-wage workers
    - progressive and conservative values support a safety net for people who work hard and play by the rules
- elaboration
  - evidence for reasons
    - empirical research on tax burden, job patterns, household demographics, and assets of low-wage workers
  - evidence for assumptions

- □ legislative history showing intent of original EITC legislation and amendments from 1975 to present [see Example 3, chapter 5]
- □ policy analysis of tax code [see Example 3, chapter 4]
- □ political analysis of values (e.g., equity, efficiency, role of government) [see Example 3, chapter 4]
- limits
  - political climate at the time of introducing a proposal to expand EITC
  - if adopted, speed of implementation (might impact other anti-poverty programs)
  - coverage (recommended solution does not cover single workers who are noncustodial parents)
  - anticipated reactions:
    - □ cooperative (others might propose compatible policy changes, such as providing incentives for businesses to offer infant day care)
    - □ competitive (others might argue that there are more pressing priorities, or there are better policy instruments, or for a different solution)
    - □ different assumptions (replace the present tax code with a flat tax)
    - □ challenges (need more empirical research and policy analysis before concluding that the tax code is unfair to low-wage workers)

## Summary and Preview

Persuasive policy argument is purposeful, critical, credible, and authoritative. This chapter tells you that positions supported by argument are more persuasive than unsupported opinion. It shows you how to argue policy positions logically and how to logically analyze positions other than your own. Chapter 7, next, applies argument to requesting action.

# References

Coplin, W. D., and M. K. O'Leary. 1998. *Public policy skills*. 3rd ed. Washington, DC: Policy Studies Associates.

Gitterman, Daniel P. 2003. Tax credits for working families. http://www. brookings.edu/reports/2003/08childrenfamilies_gitterman.aspx

Gitterman, Daniel P., Lucy S. Gorham, and Jessica L. Dorrance. 2008. Expanding the EITC for single workers and couples without children: Tax relief for all low-wage workers. *Georgetown Journal on Poverty Law and Policy*: 15, 2, 245–84.

# Further Reading

Toulmin, S. 1958. *The uses of argument*. New York: Cambridge University Press.

✦◯

# CHAPTER 7

# Petitions and Proposals:
# Request Action or Propose Policy

## Key Concepts

- getting government to act on your concern
- requesting administrative action
- proposing legislative action

Nongovernmental groups, as well as individuals, may request government action or propose public policy. Professionals in government may do so, too. This chapter shows you how to petition or propose in order to achieve policy change.

In the United States, only elected legislators are authorized to enact laws. However, requests for action and policy proposals may originate inside or outside government. While it is true that legislators or administrators originate most proposals, any citizen or group can petition for action or propose policy. Examples at the end of this chapter illustrate the variety of originators.

One longstanding practice for requesting action is petitioning. The First Amendment to the U.S. Constitution guarantees citizens' right to "petition for a redress of grievances." Over time, petitioners have come to include not only individual citizens but also groups, organizations, and corporations of many kinds. Petitioning has extended beyond redressing grievances to requesting varied actions.

To illustrate petitioning, in a case of injury experienced during air bag deployment in an automobile collision, three different petitions for government action might be made.

1. A victim of chemical burns or breathing disorders attributable to air bag deployment might petition his or her congressional representatives to amend the National Traffic and Motor Vehicle Safety Act of 1966 to authorize medical training programs specific to air bags for emergency services personnel.
2. A company that has developed a new technology for increasing passenger safety without relying solely on passenger restraints, such as air bags or safety belts, might petition the National Highway Traffic Safety Administration to test the new technology.
3. A professional association of automotive engineers might petition the National Highway Traffic Safety Administration to amend a vehicle safety design standard to include warning systems in cars to encourage seat belt use.

The other common practice for requesting action is proposing policy. External proposals usually represent organized, or group, interest in solving a problem. The role of nongovernmental groups in North American public policy making has deep historical roots. In colonial America, before the United States or its government was established, voluntary associations flourished. Individuals formed associations to provide basic social services, to meet public needs, and to protect community interests. Voluntary fire companies, water companies, library associations, prison associations, school associations, landowner associations, and militias were so common in the America of the early 1800s that a visitor from France, Alexis de Tocqueville (1945), observed,

> Americans of all ages, all conditions, and all dispositions constantly form associations.... Wherever at the head of some new undertaking you see the government in France, or a man of rank in England, in the United States you will be sure to find an association. (p. 106)

Such group activism provides background for the Tenth Amendment regarding limitations on central government that states "the powers not delegated to the United States by the Constitution, nor prohibited to it by the States, are reserved to the States respectively, or to the people."

Nowadays, groups that perform a public good might be granted tax-exempt status as nonprofit organizations. Their function might be religious, scientific, literary, educational, promotional, protective, political, charitable, or other, in accordance with Internal Revenue Service standards for 20 categories of tax-exempt activity (Internal Revenue Service 2002).

Many (possibly most) nonprofit organizations are not concerned with public policy. However, significant numbers of such groups actively try to influence the direction public policy takes. These are known as advocacy groups. Their methods vary according to the limitations of their tax-exempt status. Some limit their activity to education. These educate their members, the larger public, and the government regarding issues, but they do not lobby or support candidates for election. Their communications include legislative alerts, editorials, letters, personal visits to lawmakers, witness testimony, and more. Others, with more restricted tax benefits, might campaign for candidates running for office or lobby for outcomes of a process or provide lawmakers with expert information and political assessments and, on occasion, drafts of legislation.

Legislators often appreciate the help of advocacy groups in educating the public about needs for policy. Government staffs appreciate informed, accurate, well-argued lobbying because it helps them to brief legislators on complex or controversial issues. And, legislation and regulation writers might also appreciate proposed wording. (Example 1, this chapter, illustrates.) A positive example of public good resulting from such help might be the continued strengthening of legislation in the United States on smoking as a health problem. Past legislation on smoking has been passed in large part because health care advocacy groups worked with responsive legislators at all levels of government and educated the public to support directed warning labels on cigarettes, nonsmoking restaurant sections, and smoke-free public facilities. A negative example is the influence of lobbying by corporations and advocacy groups to weaken laws on occupational health and safety or on environmental protection.

The milk labeling case in chapter 1 exemplifies both positive and negative lobbying.

Grassroots organizations such as neighborhood or block associations, community clubs, workplace voluntary groups, and student organizations might also use petitioning or proposing to accomplish their advocacy, just as nonprofit organizations might.

Why are petitioning and proposing important? They sustain democracy; they are democratic ways of addressing public problems by institutional means. Whether by direct democracy (as with California's state referenda) or by representative democracy (as with Washington's federal legislation), self-governing society relies on procedures for public intervention in the process. Recall that public policy has far-reaching effects in the everyday life of society. Policy makers need and want information that can solve problems and build public support for action. Nongovernmental groups or individuals who are informed about the impact of a problem or a policy are excellent sources of information. So are groups or individuals who recognize a need for policy. Who petitions and proposes? Individuals can do so, but petitions and proposals by organized groups are likely to be more influential because they represent the power of collective interest.

## How to Petition for Action or Propose Policy on Behalf of a Group

*Goal:* Knowledge of the functions of nongovernmental organizations in public policy processes, and familiarity with nonprofit organizations active in your area of interest.

*Objective:* Petitioning or proposing on behalf of an organization or group.

*Product:* Brief written petition or policy proposal representing an organization's advocacy. Length varies according to purposes and situations, but a short document (one to three pages) is preferred. Genre may be prescribed or chosen. A letter is a common choice.

*Scope:* Content of group's charter, purpose, or mission will determine the concerns or issues you will address.

*Strategy:* Create a petition or proposal including the following information:

- Desired outcome: What do you want to accomplish? Can you describe it as if it were already accomplished in a future you want to achieve?

- Today's situation: What's wrong in the present? Why is the action you propose needed? What causes the need?

- Relevant background: How did the problem arise? What original assumptions are no longer valid? What conditions have changed?

- Available options: What are the alternative ways of meeting the need? Advantages and disadvantages of each? Costs (money, other) of each?

- Recommended action: What is the best alternative? Can you briefly argue as to why?

- Summary: What are the results (referring to the desired future) if requested action is performed?

- Action items: Who is asked to do what, when, where, and how?

## Task #1. Name the need, and specify the action and agency.

*Identify a need for policy:* If you already know the need you will address or the option you will advocate, proceed to the next step, specifying the desired action and the responsible agency.

If you do not know the need well, or if you have not decided on an option or you are responsible for selecting among many competing needs and options, step back to focus before you proceed. Start again wherever you need to start, whether it is to define the problem and pinpoint the issue (discovery), review the history of action or inaction (legislative history), review the arguments (the range of positions), or use the Method in chapter 2 to reconsider the policy context and the communication situation for your proposal.

*Specify the action and agency:* Determining the needed action—knowing what is possible, knowing whom to ask, and knowing what to ask for—is not simple. Much time and effort can be wasted in seeking unlikely action or making a proposal to the wrong recipient. The best way is to continually and iteratively ask and answer, "What am I trying to do?" and "How can I do it most effectively?" That will lead to further guiding questions such as "Should I start small (that is, local), or should I start big (national or international)?"

Consider the options for action; for example, choose government action. What do you want the government to do? Government can legislate, spend, regulate, and enforce, all within limits. Which type of action is needed for the problem you are concerned about? To which level of government—federal, state, local—should you direct your proposal? Which department or agency can do what you want to accomplish?

Now consider nongovernmental options. Does the solution require government action at all? For example, a citizens group might choose to organize a boycott or initiate a lawsuit to solve a civic problem rather than to ask for government action or propose public policy. Similarly, a student group might choose a community solution rather than governmental action. For example, in response to a racist incident on campus, one student group developed a constructive plan for educating students about everyday racism in campus life. Rather than proposing it as a policy to the student governance or to the school's administration, the group circulated their plan among other campus organizations and sent it to national student associations. They communicated it by word of mouth and publicized it through news media. The strategy was to ask similar student groups nationwide to draw public attention to the problem of race-based harassment on their campus and to offer as a model the original group's plan for addressing it. In this example, change in human behavior was sought through organized community education.

## Task #2. Identify the organizations active on your issue.

Here are some ways of locating and identifying nonprofit organizations:

- Check the local phone directory, or ask local volunteer services about local nonprofits or local affiliates of national and international nonprofits.

- Ask a librarian for print or online guides to nonprofit organizations. (Chapter 5 on legislative records research includes a reminder that research librarians are a real resource for communicators. A reference librarian specializing in management and business, for example, will know the latest print and online sources of information on nonprofit organizations.)

- Read the transcripts of congressional hearings on your issue to find witnesses who spoke on behalf of advocacy groups. (To find hearings, see chapter 5 on legislative history and chapter 9 on witness testimony.)
- Search newspaper databases for news articles on your issue that might refer to advocacy groups.
- Search World Wide Web portals to nonprofit organizations. Some offer free searchable lists of nonprofits such as the following:
  - Nonprofit Online News—http://news.gilbert.org
  - Urban Institute National Center for Charitable Statistics Nonprofit FAQ—http://nccsdataweb.urban.org/PubApps/nonprofitfaq.php
  - Nonprofit Yellow Pages—http://www.nonprofityellowpages.org/ypsearch.asp
  - idealist.org—http://www.idealist.org
  - Independent Sector—http://www.independentsector.org
  - The Foundation Directory Online—http://lnps.fdncenter.org
  - Guidestar—http://www.guidestar.org

Why restrict your knowledge to that provided by nonprofit organizations? You should not necessarily limit your knowledge to a single kind of source. If, for example, you represent a health care organization and are advocating for the right to use a controversial drug, you may want to enlist the support of the pharmaceutical company that manufactures the drug. While the company has a vested interest, it also might have facts and figures that could bolster or undercut your arguments. As another example, if you are advocating for highway safety improvement, you might consult with both nonprofit and for-profit experts in accident research, such as the petitioners in Examples 1 and 2 (this chapter).

## Task #3. Write.

*Absolutely key* in petitioning and in proposing is providing only accurate information. Anything else will destroy your or your organization's credibility and persuasiveness.

Use the Method in chapter 2 to prepare, plan, and produce a written petition or proposal. The document's contents should answer the questions listed under *Strategy in this* chapter. Compare the finished product to expected standards (Checklists, chapter 2).

There is no typical format for policy proposals. If you are writing for an organization that prescribes a template for policy proposals, or if your intended recipient prescribes a template, you should use it. If no template is prescribed, choose a form that is appropriate for your situation. For any written document requesting government action, the conventions of professional communication will apply. Identify the presenter and recipient, summarize in an overview, and organize content in subheaded sections. The document type might be a letter, a memo, a full-page ad in print newspapers, animated ads in online newspapers, a public declaration dramatically delivered in historical costume, a YouTube video, or another form chosen for its effectiveness in the situation. See, for example, the websites of national nonprofit groups that sometimes express their advocacy in funny as well as serious and attention-grabbing ways.

## Five Examples

These examples show petitioning and proposing by professionals inside and outside government.

### *Example 1. Petition*

**Center for Auto Safety**
1825 Connecticut Avenue, NW #33a
Washington, DC 20009–5708 (202) 328–1770
www.autosafety.org
January 21, 2007
The Honorable Nicole R. Nason, Administrator
National Highway Traffic Safety Administration
400 Seventh Street, SM7
Washington, DC 20590

**Petition for Rulemaking**
Dear Ms. Nason:

   The Center for Auto Safety (CAS) petitions the National Highway Traffic Safety Administration (NHTSA) to take action to restrict the availability of two-way communication features through in-vehicle telematic systems while a vehicle is in motion. The purpose of this petition is to make the driving environment safer by reducing the availability of devices that have been proven to be traffic hazards.

According to NHTSA spokesman Rae Tyson, "Our recommendation is that you should not talk on the phone while driving, whether it's a hand-held or hands-free device." It is time for NHTSA to put the results of extensive research and its own recommendation into action.

## Background

The automotive industry has long been aware of the dangers posed by talking on a cell phone while operating a motor vehicle. Cellular telephones are an important resource for drivers who encounter emergency situations and pull off the road to make calls. However, when cell phones are used while driving, they are a significant cause of highway crashes. Many existing in-vehicle technologies…are being expanded to offer cellular telephone service to drivers. What was once an essentially helpful technology is becoming a source of dangerous driver distraction by the addition of personal communication features that are available to a person while driving.

In search of new profit centers, major auto companies are marketing vehicle-in-motion telematic options that degrade the safety value of the Automatic Crash Notification (ACN) originally installed in motor vehicles. For example, General Motors, which was a leader in ACN with its OnStar system, began degrading safety by including personal cell phone use as an integral part of OnStar. GM once tried expanding the scope of in-vehicle telematic systems to allow drivers to receive email, movie listings, personalized news, sport reports and weather while driving. The potential distraction is similar to permitting television monitors in the front seats of passenger vehicles, a practice that is *not* permitted by state law in most, if not all states.

...

## Research Studies

Research has consistently shown that operating a motor vehicle while talking on a cell phone, whether hand-held or hands-free, increases the risk of an accident to three or four times the experience of attentive drivers. The general consensus of the scientific community is that there is little, if any, difference in crash rates involving hands-free versus hand-held cell phones. The two-way conversation on a cellular phone, not the task of holding the phone, causes a cognitive distraction. This distraction induces "inattention blindness," inhibiting drivers' abilities to detect change in road conditions.

## State Legislation

...

The highest standard enacted by District of Columbia, Connecticut, New Jersey and New York prohibits the use of any handheld cellular phone but permits drivers to use hands-free wireless devices.

...

Many cities have encountered difficulty enforcing bans because of the high number of violations....The total number of cell phone calls from 1996–2001, 326 billion, shows the enormous potential exposure of cell phone use in vehicles.

...

### Exemplary Vehicle Crashes

No one can deny that cell phones have resulted in traffic crashes, deaths, and injuries. [Name] and [Name] were both killed when drivers talking on cell phones struck their vehicles while they were stopped at a stop light.

...There are hundreds of cases like [theirs]...NHTSA has known from the time of the first head of the agency, William Haddon, MD, that the best public health strategy is one that is passive; in this case, not permitting cell phone technology to be so readily available.

### Conclusion

...

It is time for the government to intervene on this dangerous practice...As a first step, the Center petitions NHTSA to issue a notice of proposed rulemaking which would amend FMVVSS102 to add a new provision reading:

*Any vehicle integrated personal communication systems including cellular phones and text-messaging systems shall be inoperative when the transmission shift lever is in a forward or reverse position.*

...

Sincerely,
Clarence M. Ditlow, Executive Director
Tyler Patterson, Vehicle Safety Intern

(The full petition can be seen at http://www.regulations.gov)
Docket ID: NHTSA-2007–28442
Document ID: NHTSA-2007–28442-0003
Date Posted: Sep 13, 2007)

### *Example 2. Petition*

In the late 1990s, two professionals in auto safety created a for-profit corporation in the public interest to assist victims in litigation resulting from automobile accidents. Both are experts, one of them in highway safety policy and the other in automobile design for occupant safety. Concerned about the high rates of injury and fatality caused in part by drivers' and passengers' failure to use seat belts, the experts frequently petitioned the responsible federal government agency to amend the safety standard to require inducements in all vehicles to encourage seat belt use. Here, next, is a recent letter to the agency head regarding a persistent problem. This letter refers to earlier petitions by these experts. Following, a petition on the same problem with its transmittal letter to an earlier agency head is shown.

## Letter

Carl E. Nash
(address)
(phone)
(e-mail)

February 11, 2002

The Honorable Jeffrey W. Runge, M.D.
National Highway Traffic Safety Administrator
Washington, D.C. 20590

Dear Dr. Runge:

As I promised at the Fuel Economy/Safety session of the Transportation Research Board meeting, I am enclosing copies of the petitions that Donald Friedman and I submitted to NHTSA before you became Administrator. They asked NHTSA to address the question of safety belt use inducements or reminders. We believe you, as Administrator, have considerable flexibility in how you might address this important contribution to motor vehicle safety.

NHTSA could take rulemaking action to require effective belt use reminders, but you could more expeditiously use your bully pulpit and other means to get auto makers to install more effective reminders in their new vehicles. A small research and fleet test program—which the industry should conduct along with NHTSA—could determine the most effective means of getting occupants to buckle up.

You are probably aware that the Insurance Institute for Highway Safety (IIHS) evaluated the weak reminder that has been included in most new Ford vehicles since 2000 and found that it increased usage by about five percentage points....Ford found no consumer resistance or complaints from this very innocuous reminder. A more effective reminder...could be developed with a modest research program. The safety payoff over the next decade would be quite substantial, not to mention the fact that it would free police resources now used to enforce belt use laws.

I am a strong advocate of non-regulatory approaches to automotive issues. In particular, the committee technical standards writing process of the American Society for Testing and Materials (ASTM) is highly democratic *(anyone with something to contribute can participate)*, effective *(it makes use of knowledge and expertise from all quarters)*, and fair *(it cannot be dominated by any specific interest and these committees must reach consensus)*. ASTM committees can produce consumer information standards that are objective, that meet the need for motor vehicle safety, and that are stated in performance terms. As an example, it would have been preferable to establish an (ASTM) committee to draft the side air bag standard last year.

...More comprehensive consumer information on motor vehicle safety can be an effective complement to NHTSA's minimum regulatory standards....This market-based approach is more flexible for both the government and auto makers, and can facilitate important choices by individual car buyers.

If you would like to discuss the possibilities of this approach further, I would be pleased to participate in such conversations and to recommend others with a similar interest in this approach.

With regards,
Carl E. Nash, Ph.D.
Enclosures

## Letter

Carl E. Nash
(address)
(telephone number)
(e-mail address)

December 17, 1998

The Honorable Ricardo Martinez, M.D., Administrator
National Highway Traffic Safety Administration
400 Seventh Street, SW
Washington, D.C. 20590

Dear Dr. Martinez:

Enclosed is a petition for the National Highway Traffic Safety Administration to amend Federal Motor Vehicle Safety Standard 208 to require an effective safety belt inducement in all new motor vehicles. It has been a quarter century since the unfortunate experience with safety belt ignition interlocks. You have an obligation to seriously reconsider the potential of vehicle-based systems to substantially increase belt use.

The advantages of an acceptable, effective belt use inducement are substantial. It would reduce fatalities by at least 7,000 per year and would reduce injuries comparably. It would permit the agency to respond favorably to the industry's desire that NHTSA rescind the unbelted test in FMVSS 208. It would end the controversy over the use of safety belt use laws as an excuse for stopping minority drivers.

Donald Friedman and I have also submitted comments to the docket of the advanced air bag rulemaking notice that build on the concept of an effective safety belt use inducement. We believe that a simpler and more effective approach to reducing inflation induced injuries can be based on this concept.

In the interest of advancing motor vehicle safety, we look forward to your favorable consideration of our petition and of our comments on the rulemaking proposal. Action that could make belt use nearly universal in the United States is long overdue, and would be an important legacy of your tenure.

Sincerely,
Carl E. Nash, Ph.D.

## Petition

To Amend FMVSS 208, Occupant Crash Protection To Require Effective Belt Use Inducement

Carl E. Nash, Ph.D., and Donald Friedman
Washington, D.C., and Santa Barbara, California

### Summary

This is a petition to amend Federal Motor Vehicle Safety Standard 208 (FMVSS 208) to require effective safety belt use inducement systems in all new motor vehicles sold in the United States. This requirement should become effective no later than the beginning of the 2001 model year. The inducement systems should activate only if a person sits in either front outboard seating position and does not attach the safety belt after occupying the seat and would stop when the belt is buckled. The requirement must be consistent with the "interlock" amendment to the National Traffic and Motor Vehicle Safety Act of 1966 (15 U.S.C. 1410b), which prohibits ignition interlocks and continuous buzzers.

The inducements could include, but need not be limited to: (1) a continuous visual warning to buckle safety belts located prominently on the instrument panel, (2) an intermittent, repeating audible suggestion (such as with a synthesized voice) warning occupants to buckle their safety belt, and (3) disruption of electrical power to such non-essential accessories as the radio, tape or CD player, and air conditioning. We further recommend that NHTSA undertake a quick reaction project to determine the acceptability and effectiveness of various types of use inducements to ensure that the spirit of the interlock amendment is not violated.

### Background

...

### Restraint Policy and Use Today

...

### An Amendment to FMVSS 208

Therefore, we petition NHTSA to amend FMVSS 208 to require a reasonable and effective safety belt use inducement to be built into all new vehicles. Effective belt use inducements can be required without violating the "interlock" amendment (15 U.S.C. 1410b) to the National Traffic and Motor Vehicle Safety Act...

Safety belt use is widespread, generally accepted, and required by law in virtually all states. The design for comfort and convenience of safety belts in many new vehicles has improved since the days of the interlock. Thus, we doubt that many motorists would object to use of well-designed inducement systems. However, we recommend that NHTSA conduct quick reaction tests using panels and field tests to determine effectiveness and consumer acceptance of various types of use inducements....We note that a policy of increasing belt use through an inducement built into new motor vehicles would be preferable to the present policy of safety belt use laws for reasons unrelated to safety. Civil rights organizations (most recently the Urban League) have objected to primary belt use laws because of their potential to give police officers an excuse to stop minority drivers. Having the inducement built into the vehicle takes away that issue and should be strongly supported by civil rights and civil liberties advocates.

Requiring a belt use inducement built into all new vehicles would be a major improvement in every way to FMVSS 208. As existing cars are retired from use, it would increase belt use to near universality (with the attendant reduction in fatalities and serious injuries in all crash modes) without further state laws or enforcement activities. In fact, states could sunset their safety belt use laws within the next decade or two. We estimate that a belt use inducement has the potential to save a minimum of 7,000 additional lives per year.

We urge that NHTSA give priority to both testing and simultaneous rulemaking in response to our petition.

(The full petition can be found at http://www.regulations.gov. Docket ID: NHTSA-1998–4405 Document ID: NHTSA-1998–4405-0062 Date Posted: Dec 17, 1998. For the agency's comment denying this petition see its *Federal Register* notice on advanced air bags: F.R. vol. 64, no. 214, page 60625–6. [The notice begins on page 60556]. The docket identifier is NHTSA 1999–6407-0001.)

---

**WHAT EXAMPLES 1 AND 2 SHOW** Example 1 on cell phone use is an external petition by a nonprofit organization of experts. No specific policy process is underway, which explains why the petitioners ask the agency to start the process by issuing a notice of proposed rulemaking on the subject, use of cell phones while driving, and a call for public comment. Example 2 on seat belt use, also an external petition by a for-profit organization of experts, addresses such a call.

Examples 1 and 2 illustrate in-depth presentation of information. They are written to be read silently, not spoken aloud. One cue to this intention is the length of sentences in both texts. Many sentences in Examples 1 and 2 would cause a speaker to run out of breath. Another cue is the extensive detail.

The amount of detail in Examples 1 and 2 is probably appropriate. For both petitions and proposals, as for funding requests, the contents and length of submissions might be prescribed by the receiving agency. If the agency prescribes the information and length it wants and the form it prefers, write accordingly. Otherwise, a petition or proposal, like a grant application, might go unconsidered.

Where to put all the details? Putting them in the main body of the document can be an unwise choice. Detailed explanation or historical background can bury the message. A potential choice for the writers of Example 2 on seat belt use is to put explanation, background, and critique in an appendix. The success of this option depends on the circumstances of reception. To decide whether to append supporting information, writers need to understand the readers' situation. If all readers will receive the whole document and if they are willing to flip between the main text and appendix as they read, writers can safely choose to append detailed information. However, in some policy work settings, readers are likely to receive not the whole document but only the parts that pertain to their jurisdiction or responsibility. Appended information might not reach them. It is perhaps for this reason that the writers of Example 2 knowingly chose not to use appendices.

Examples 1 and 2 are well organized for readability. Document structure aids rapid comprehension. Even so, the message could be emphasized more in Example 2. Within paragraphs, the petitioners' implicit message ("There is a better way") competes with the implied critique ("The agency's way is flawed"). Impatient readers might want a sharper focus on the message.

### Example 3. Petition

The Agriculture Marketing Services of the U.S. Department of Agriculture (USDA) "facilitate the domestic and international marketing of U.S. agricultural products...ensure the health and care of animals and plants...[and participate in] setting national and international standards" (http://www.ams.usda.gov). A tool of this service is the marketing agreement, which is a legal agreement "designed to stabilize market conditions for certain agricultural commodities by regulating the handling of those commodities in interstate or foreign commerce" (http://www.nationalaglawcenter.org/assets/overviews/marketingorders.html). In 2009, vegetable growers in western states petitioned the USDA to create a marketing agreement. The petitioner, an agriculture trade association, advocated solving the vegetable safety problem through a public-private partnership of government and industry. In effect, the petitioners asked to use market management as a policy mechanism. Elsewhere in this guide, you can read critiques of this approach by other agriculture advocates who recommended strengthening the FDA's food supply regulatory authority (Example 4, chapter 3; Example 1, chapter 4; Example 4, chapter 10).

## Letter

Rayne Pegg, Administrator
US Department of Agriculture Agricultural Marketing Service
1400 Independence Avenue, SW, Room 3170-S Washington, DC 20250–0247

### Re: Proposed Federal Marketing Agreement for Leafy Green Vegetables

Dear Administrator Pegg:

On June 8, 2009 a coalition of proponents petitioned the United States Department of Agriculture's Agricultural Marketing Service (AMS) to establish a national marketing agreement for leafy greens. We declared our interest in pursuing an agreement believing that such a program "would provide a clear and logical framework for signatory handlers to improve the quality of U.S. and imported leafy green products" and that it would "…empower industry representatives to engage proactively with USDA, the US Food and Drug Administration (FDA), and others in the development of production and handling practices…"

Along with our letter requesting AMS' consideration of a national agreement we submitted DRAFT language and other documentation to support our petition. Since that time we have begun to get feedback on the DRAFT as it was proposed. We understand that both proponents and USDA will receive continuous feedback throughout the process of debating and developing a national marketing agreement. In the short period since our request we have received several comments and questions that if incorporated or addressed in the DRAFT would result in an improved document. Key among these are an expanded set of definitions, several clarifications of language as well as minor modifications to include representatives of Environmental Protection Agency (USEPA) on the Technical Review Board and ensure periodic review of any established audit metrics.

We believe these modifications improve on the submitted DRAFT and are offering this revised version in advance of any federal register notice in the hopes that this DRAFT will gain broader acceptance. As proponents we are committed to ensuring the development and acceptance of a national marketing agreement that meets the diverse needs of the industry, regulatory partners and public at large. We have a common goal in advancing a program that will increase the quality of leafy greens by enhancing our ability to minimize the potential for microbial contamination. We remain committed to working collaboratively with all stakeholders to achieve that goal.

Sincerely,

United Fresh Produce Association; Produce Marketing Association; Georgia Fresh Vegetable Association; Georgia Farm Bureau; Texas Vegetable Association; Arizona Farm Bureau; Leafy Greens Council; California Farm Bureau Federation; California Leafy Green Products Handler Marketing Agreement Grower-Shipper Association of Central California; Western Growers Imperial Valley; Vegetable Growers Association

CC. David Shipman, Associate Administrator, AMS Robert Keeney, Deputy Administrator, Fruit and Vegetable Programs, AMS Mike Durando, Branch Chief, Marketing Order Administration Branch, AMS

## Petition

### *JUSTIFICATION OF PROPOSED FEDERAL MARKETING AGREEMENT FOR LEAFY GREEN VEGETABLES*

#### 1. What is the purpose of the proposal?

The proposed national leafy green marketing agreement (NLGMA) program would be a voluntary program that would provide a clear and logical framework for signatory handlers to improve the quality of U.S. and imported leafy green products. A national leafy greens marketing agreement would empower industry representatives to engage proactively with USDA, the US Food and Drug Administration (FDA), and others in the development of production and handling practices (best practices, or metrics). Formation of these best practices within the agreement framework would ensure the adoption of science-based, scalable, and regionally flexible metrics in conformance with the FDA's Good Agricultural Practices (GAPs), Good Handling Practices (GHPs) and Good Manufacturing Practices (GMPs). Coupled with a corresponding audit-based verification program, these best practices would minimize microbial contamination of fresh leafy green vegetables in the growing and handling processes, enhance the overall quality of fresh product in the marketplace, and boost public confidence in these commodities. Ultimately, an agreement would support the marketability of fresh leafy green vegetables and overall stability of the industry.

Therefore, the proposed marketing agreement would:

- Provide a mechanism to enable leafy green handlers to organize;
- Enhance the quality of fresh leafy green vegetable products available in the marketplace through the application of good agricultural production and handling practices;
- Implement a uniform, auditable, science-based food quality enhancement program;
- Provide for USDA validation and verification of program compliance;
- Foster greater collaboration with local, state and federal regulators; improve consumer confidence in leafy greens.

## 2. What problem is the proposal designed to address? Explain/quantify.

The proposed program is designed to minimize microbial contamination in the production and handling of fresh leafy green vegetables placed in the marketplace for human consumption...

...

More than 10,000 foodborne disease outbreaks were reported to the Centers for Disease Control and Prevention (CDC) foodborne disease outbreak surveillance system from 1973–2006. Researchers there discovered that approximately 5 percent of those foodborne outbreaks were linked to consumption of leafy greens...

Because some of the outbreaks were widespread, the contamination quite possibly occurred early in the production process—either at the farm level or the processing plant. Although there are more outbreaks of foodborne illness caused by seafood, more people get sick when produce is the source of contamination....

### Figure 1: Foodborne illness related to fresh produce

Source: Center for Science in the Public Interest

### Figure 2: Average Illnesses per Outbreak by Category 1998–2006

Source: Center for Science in the Public Interest

### Figure 3: Average Illnesses of *E. Coli* Outbreaks by Category 1998–2006

Source: Center for Science in the Public Interest

[Figures are omitted here because of space limitations.]

## 3. What are the current requirements or industry practices relative to the proposal?

Overview of Current Fresh Leafy Green Industry Quality and Food Safety Requirements in the U.S.

Producers and most handling operations in the leafy green industry are not regulated in the U.S.; however processing facilities are regulated by the federal government under Title 21, Part 110 of the Code of Federal Regulations. This section highlights the voluntary programs for leafy greens that exist at both the state and federal level....Lastly, there are requirements imposed by buyers that are a necessity for access to certain markets.

...

### Food Safety Guidance Documents

Nationally, there are no government audited, enforceable food safety requirements for the growing or handling of leafy green vegetables with the exception of processing facilities that are subject to current good manufacturing practices as outlined in Title 21, Part 110 of the Code of Federal Regulations. Two guidance documents developed by the government and the industry provide guidelines for best practices in the fresh produce industry and leafy green supply chain as indicated below.

- FDA and USDA Guidance to Industry—Guide to Minimize Microbial Food Safety Hazards for Fresh Fruits and Vegetables
  ...
- Commodity Specific Food Safety Guidelines for the Lettuce and Leafy Greens Supply Chain

...

### Marketing Agreements in California and Arizona

The leafy green marketing agreements, governing fresh leafy greens in Arizona and California respectively, are voluntary programs; however, the requirements of those agreements are mandatory for all signatory handlers/shippers. Signatories have an annual audit conducted by their state's department of agriculture for food safety issues. Participation is renewed on an annual basis.

...

### Buyer Requirements

Currently there are many different food safety and quality requirements levied from the retail and food service industries on leafy greens producers and handlers. Today, handlers, including those who have signed on to the Arizona and California marketing agreements, are subject to many different requirements from the retail and food service industries. Buyers may develop their own quality and safety standards or adopt established systems such as the Global Food Safety Initiative standards. Some of these requirements are very costly to implement. This has not deterred the industry from paying for and adding on another layer of GAPs as mandated by these agreements. If a handler does not abide by buyer requirements, their leafy greens products would not be introduced into commerce and could result in a grave economic loss for the handler and grower.

A national marketing agreement would establish consistency in leafy green production and handling practices through the industry supply chain. This would help to mitigate the costs of multiple quality and food safety requirements since buyers do not need to audit producers' production practices as often, and buyers will be less likely to require producers to adopt practices in addition to those included in the national agreement.

...

(The full petition with transmittal letters can be found at http://www.ams.usda.gov/AMSv1.0/getfile?dDocName=STELPRDC5077207.)

---

**WHAT EXAMPLES 2 AND 3 SHOW**  Petitioners use varied forms of documentation to request administrative action. As Example 1 shows, a letter alone might be sufficient. Alternatively, letters might introduce an accompanying petition document as in Examples 2 and 3. Introductory or transmittal letters do just that, introduce; they do not develop the petitioner's position and its supporting argument. The accompanying documentation does that.

Managing a suite of communications, even a small suite like a letter and an accompanying document, requires skill. The petitioners in Examples 2 and 3 demonstrate skill. In Example 3, the letter states the petitioner's position, then the justification section of the longer document develops it in detail.

The justification's content is organized as answers to prescribed questions. The petitioner must answer the required questions. Craft is sometimes needed to wedge multiple kinds of evidence, nuanced argument, and accountability into answers (possibly with word limits) to required questions. (Academic exam-takers know this from experience, as do grant proposal writers.) Question-and-answer format is common in governmental interaction, both written and spoken. Policy communicators need the capability of answering questions knowledgeably, strategically, and ethically. These examples demonstrate techniques of allocation, condensation, and cueing the reader for careful reading. (Additional techniques are described in chapter 9 on testifying in a public hearing.)

In Example 3, the variety of evidence types illustrates the petitioner's knowledge of the domain, vegetable growing and handling, and of the problem, foodborne illness attributed to leafy vegetables. Ample detail and consideration of multiple stakeholder perspectives serve as rhetorical devices, too. They help to convince recipients that the presenter is informed and has a balanced perspective. In Example 3, the petition's rhetorical purpose is to convince recipients in the USDA and other federal agencies (as well as skeptical vegetable growers) that the industry can self-regulate to meet safety standards set in cooperation with the USDA. Example 2 argues similarly regarding the automobile industry and the NHTSA. Each exemplifies skilled use of the genre, petitioning, to persuade government to do what the petitioner wants.

## *Example 4. Proposal*

### Scenario

Senior officers in the Surgeon General's Office have decided that another attempt to increase Reserve Armed Force eligibility for health care is justified. More frequent, longer lasting active deployments, increasing injury rates, and depleted state budgets for reservists' benefits motivate the new effort. The Chief of Patient Information has been persuasive, too. As anticipated, she is now tasked to write the necessary legislative documents. Collaboration with other specialist staff will be necessary. For example, as specialist for eligibility, she will gather dollar information and other numbers from the medical budget staff. When all information is in hand, she drafts a prescribed strategic planning document called a Unified Legislative and Budgeting Initiative. Before it can be submitted to her immediate supervisor, all the peer specialists in her office with whom she has consulted will review the draft. Upon submission, it will be reviewed by an eight-level chain of command beginning with her immediate supervisor, going on to the Secretary of the Army and all applicable staff experts, congressional liaison, and legal opinion to conclude, if necessary, with the Secretary of Defense. Any level of review may request changes, which she will make and then re-submit to the requesting reviewer.

*FY 2011 Legislative Initiative*
(Unified Legislation and Budgeting)

*TITLE*
*Increase the Early Eligibility (EE) Period for TRICARE Benefits for Members of the Reserve Components*

### Short Proposal Description
To initiate a Unified Legislation and Budgeting (ULB) proposal to enable Reserve Components to address the Secretary of Defense's changes to mobilization policy. Under this proposal, the effective date for the entitlement to early TRICARE benefits for members of the Reserve Components receiving alert orders to active duty would be the date of the issuance of the alert order. Current law only provides 90 days of early TRICARE benefits for members of the Reserve Components. The current 90 day authorization does not provide sufficient advanced notice to allow Reserve Component members to take advantage of this benefit. This ULB does not propose a change to TRICARE coverage for military dependents or family members.

### Approximate Full Year Cost ($M)
The current cost of this benefit to the government is $---- per service member, per year.

. . .

### Discussion of Requirement and Relationship to HR Strategy
After a member is identified, screened and determined to be qualified for deployment, on average, he or she has a short time to take

advantage of the Early Eligibility Period for TRICARE Benefits. If a member of the Reserve Components is identified as non-deployable due to a medical issue, the current 90-day TRICARE benefit does not provide adequate time for the medical issue to be treated. Additionally, the current benefit does not allow a service member adequate time to rehabilitate after medical treatment, thus eliminating a pool of otherwise deployable resources. As a result, the Reserve Components are overrun with service members who are unable to mobilize, leaving unit readiness diminished dramatically.

Providing an early TRICARE benefit upon the receipt of an alert order to active duty would allow for the treatment, rehabilitation, and successful mobilization for countless service members. This benefit will enable the fullest utilization of the service member's training and experience, to ensure higher levels of unit readiness. Extending this benefit will also solidify unit cohesion and allow the Reserve Components to be more responsive to wartime requirements.

This proposal would allow Reserve Component service members the maximum use of Early Eligibility for TRICARE. Increasing the eligibility period in coordination with other Reserve Component initiatives for earlier alert notification will result in higher unit readiness and higher retention of service members.

### Business Case

Reserve Component service members do not currently have adequate time to utilize this benefit to identify, treat, and rehabilitate medically disqualifying issues prior to mobilization. This has a tremendous adverse impact not only on service members and their families, but more importantly, on unit readiness and national defense.

This proposal directly supports the Army Legislative Objective to reset the Force to ensure readiness for current and future challenges with full funding to restore units to levels of readiness required to successfully execute programmed operational deployments, future contingencies, and homeland defense missions.

This proposal will enable the reserve component service members to receive preventive care and treatments necessary to become fully medically ready. Extending this benefit to alert to mobilization will allow ample time during the Reset/Train Pool of the ARFORGEN cycle to increase the readiness percentage and bring the RAF force to a green status. In addition, this will allow leadership to focus on training, mobilization activities, increase unit readiness and most importantly increase the quality of life for the service member. DOD has a high interest is seeing a fully deployable RAF force.

All seven Reserve Components have a direct stake in seeing a change in the legislation for this benefit. The Army National Guard, the Air National Guard, the Army Reserves, the Air Force Reserves, the Marine Reserves, the Coast Guard Reserves, and the Naval Reserves would be greatly impacted.

**Number of Personnel Affected**

|        | Army   | Navy  | Marine Corps | Air Force |
|--------|--------|-------|--------------|-----------|
| Number | 54,000 | 6,000 | 4,000        | 12,000    |

*Resource Requirement ($M)*
The Early Eligibility for Medical Benefits (EE) is funded by the Defense Health Program Association Fund. Due to limited resources, the RAF does not have funding for this proposal.

...

**Note:** This proposal requires a corresponding appropriation of funding for implementation.

*Cost Methodology*
Cost factors include 76,000 Reserve Component service members mobilized annually. The current cost of this benefit to the government is $—per service member. (This data is based on the GAO TRICARE Reserve Select report 08–104, December 2007.) Currently there are 38,700 Soldiers deployed and eligible for this benefit. The estimated funding impact to provide twelve months worth of the EE benefit is $—M.

### Legislative Language

Current Public Law 108–136, National Defense Authorization Act for Fiscal Year 2004, section 703 states "a member of the Reserve Components who is issued a delayed-effective date active duty order or is covered by such an order for a period of active duty of more than 30 days, in support of a contingency operation, as defined in 10 U.S.C. 101(a)(13)(B)., shall be eligible, along with the member's dependents, for TRICARE, on either the date of issuance of such an order, or 90 days prior to the date the active duty prescribed in the order, whichever is later."

This proposal will change Public Law 108–136 section 703 to read "...the effective date of active duty for purposes of entitlement to active duty health care of members of the Reserve Components of the Armed Forces receiving alert order anticipating a call or order to active duty in support of a contingency operation, shall be the date of the issuance of the alert order for the member's unit in anticipation of the mobilization of the unit for service for a period of more than 30 days in support of a contingency operation or the date of the issuance of the order providing for the assignment or attachment of the member to a unit subject to an alert order. The member's dependents shall be eligible for TRICARE 90 days prior to the date of active duty prescribed in the order."

This proposal does not impact any other section of the law.

### Sectional Analysis

*Pros*

The proposal will dramatically improve medical readiness by allowing maximum time to identify and treat medical issues that may affect unit readiness and deployability.

Service members will have an increased ability to use the TRICARE Benefit throughout the entire alert period to identify and treat medical issues and to fully rehabilitate after medical treatment. This will ensure that Reserve Component units will be at a higher state of readiness and ensure the full use of each service member's skills and training.

*Cons*

The cost of this proposal is over $---- million over a five-year period. The RAF does not have funding for this proposal.

*Example 5. Proposal*

---

### Scenario

An undergraduate student is a longtime volunteer in a local women's center that participates in a statewide coalition of private and public groups concerned about domestic violence. As a volunteer supporting the center's small administrative staff, the student is often given writing tasks. She has produced public information documents including brochures, guides to services, and how-to instructions. This time, her supervisor asks her to draft a policy statement on the center's advocacy for amending proposed legislation regarding guns and domestic abuse. The center director will present the statement in a public hearing on the legislation.

---

### *Policy Proposal*

#### Who I Represent

For the past 20 years the Maryland Network Against Domestic Violence (MNADV) has been working to end domestic violence against women. MNADV works with domestic violence service providers and criminal justice personnel throughout the state to provide consistent community responses to domestic violence. In support of community response, MNADV focuses its lobbying efforts on changes needed in state law and has aided in passing almost thirty pieces of domestic violence legislation. Currently, we support the passage of HB1 46 Domestic Violence Protective Order Additional Relief. This legislation provides for legal procedures requiring domestic abusers to surrender firearms after a protective order hearing.

#### Our Position

The issue is whether a person who has been accused of an act of domestic violence should be allowed to own firearms. As a representative for MNADV, I am here to say that we strongly feel that keeping guns out of the hands of batterers will help prevent further physical injury to victims. In Maryland, the majority of domestic violence incidents involve a gun or other firearm.

Currently, Maryland has no law that keeps guns away from batterers. As a result, men who are convicted of domestic violence often end up going back to their victims, with a gun, when their sentence is over. If Maryland does not pass a law preventing batterers from owning firearms, victims who have survived are more likely to become victims again. If Maryland fails to pass such a law, the state is also failing to adequately protect abused women.

If a person convicted of or accused of domestic violence is charged with a misdemeanor for owning a firearm as HB 146 provides, the number of deaths due to guns in the case of domestic violence will be lowered.

---

•— **WHAT EXAMPLES 4 AND 5 SHOW** Example 4 on military health care is an internal proposal by a professional in government. Example 5 on domestic violence is an external proposal by a volunteer in a nonprofit organization.

Example 4 shows use of a prescribed template for proposing legislation, while Example 5 shows an individually chosen form for making a public statement of advocacy. Example 4's pared-down style utilizes graphic devices, whereas Example 5's plain style utilizes to-the-point exposition. Each style fits its document's purpose and cultural context.

Because it is intended for oral delivery, possibly in a one- or two-minute summary, Example 5 on domestic violence is compact. It includes only the message and key evidence. In a public hearing, as in a briefing, time limitations usually force the omission of details from the oral statement. Details can be presented later in the hearing during question-and-answer. Details can be read, also, in the full written statement that is usually provided to the agency or committee holding the hearing. Additionally, a staff member for the hearing's convener might follow up by asking the organization's witness for more information.

Example 4 on military health care is intended to be read and discussed in meetings by people familiar with the genre, unified legislative and budgeting initiative, and with the subject, soldiers' health care needs. Consequently, it does not explain specialized terms such as TRICARE (current military health plan) or abbreviations such as FY2011 (fiscal year 2011).

Example 4's argument is strongly supported by evidence of need, examination of assumptions, legislative analysis, political analysis, and cost estimation.

All these examples are credible. Each, for its purpose, informs sufficiently and organizes content readably. Examples 4 on military health care and 5 on domestic violence do not provide accountability by naming the presenter and intended recipient in the document shown here. Likely, an accompanying cover sheet or other tracking sheet did name them.

## Summary and Preview

Requesting government action is more an art than a science. This chapter offers know-how for two common ways of requesting action, petitioning and proposing. Chapter 8, next, focuses on communication skills for briefing policy makers.

## References

Internal Revenue Service. 2002. *The digital daily.* 2 May. http:// www.irs.gov

Tocqueville, Alexis de. 1945. *Democracy in America.* Vol. 2. New York: Alfred A. Knopf. [Originally published 1840]

CHAPTER **8**

↜

# Briefing Memo or Opinion Statement: Inform Policy Makers

## Key Concepts

- brevity
- politeness
- e-mail

Policy makers need information for making decisions. They usually prefer it in short, quickly comprehended summary form. This chapter helps you to write two kinds of summary, a briefing memo and an opinion statement. It includes cautionary guidance on e-mail.

During a policy process, authorities receive large amounts of unsolicited information and advice. Often, they ignore it. Instead, they directly seek the information and advice they need.

What kinds of information or advice do policy makers typically need? For consideration of a problem, general information might include assessments of events or conditions; arguments and critical analyses of arguments; reviews of policy options and technical analyses of the options; specialized topic reports; investigative reports; summaries of laws germane to the issue; legal counsel on interpretation of laws; and summaries of expert opinion, public opinion, and political advocacy. Beyond these general types of information, any single issue demands its own particular and detailed information.

For example, a municipality that is developing a comprehensive plan for land use will need general assessments of area conditions (environmental, economic, historical, and cultural factors), reports on current costs of providing services in the area (such as roads, water, and sewage treatment), summaries of relevant state laws (such as regulations governing municipal planning), and more. To apply general information to a specific municipality (such as a township or village), its elected officials might ask county or state government agencies for local population statistics, economic projections, or environmental data. They might ask legal counsel to examine land-use planning tools, such as zoning ordinances in nearby municipalities, or to review case law on legal challenges to them. To prepare for public discussion of draft plans and ordinances, the officials will seek political advice. They will want to know the opinion and advice of organized groups and individuals living in the municipality.

Who provides information to policy makers? It varies by level of government. In federal and state governments, professional staff might produce much of the needed information. The staff's know-how, or familiarity with the policy process and understanding of the political context, enables them to inform policy makers usefully. Staff members typically write briefing memos.

Municipal government differs from federal and state government in the size of staffs. While large municipalities might be well staffed, smaller ones have small staffs, or no staff. Consequently, local elected officials might do their own information gathering. They might utilize a range of information providers including experts (representing subject knowledge), advocacy and stakeholder groups (representing organized interests), legal counsels (representing rules and procedures), other officials and associations of elected officials (representing politics), and citizens (representing the opinion or experience of individuals or groups). Any of these providers might write an opinion statement or a briefing memo to inform an official's work of representation.

A briefing memo should be terse and targeted. It provides succinct, pointed information to people who have too much to do and not enough time. Whether its topic is narrow or broad, a briefing memo offers only essentials targeted to a particular reader's need to know. As distinguished from policy analysis memos or policy briefs, which are longer and include discussion, possibly with detailed appendices, briefing memos are short and compact. They highlight, only. Expected length is one to two pages. Writers of briefing memos should design content for quick comprehension and easy referral. Pages should have a document header for targeted identification; an opening summary (not an introduction) for overview; "chunked" information with sub-headings for directing attention; shorter sentences with one main idea per sentence for emphasis, and only necessary words.

## How to Inform Policy Makers in a Briefing Memo or Opinion Statement

*Goal:* Recognition of meaningful information in a mass of details and representation.

*Objectives:* Capability of distilling, relating details to context, interpreting details accurately in context, and selecting details according to relevance. Capability of efficiently stating informed opinion that is aware of and responsive to other opinions.

*Product:* One- to two-page written briefing memo or one- to two-paragraph written opinion statement, possibly with attachments.

*Scope:* Only relevant topics in a specific context targeted to meet a particular information need.

*Strategy:* Use guiding questions to develop the document's contents. Apply all of the questions in the Method (chapter 2).

### Task #1. Develop the information

From meetings:

- attend relevant public or private meetings; take full notes; get copies of the agenda and related documents; get contact information for participants

- jot (in the margins of the agenda) your own notes and questions about the proceedings, and capture (as nearly verbatim as you can) the significant questions asked by others

- contact participants, government staff, topic experts, or knowledgeable citizens for answers to questions or referrals to other sources immediately after the meeting

From experts:

- conduct information searches for relevant research and analysis

From informed reflection and analysis:

- update original questions and reframe the issues as information develops
- pause periodically to summarize your understanding and to critically examine it
- continue to consult as needed to improve your understanding of the process and context

### Task #2. Write the memo or statement

Before you write, review the Method in chapter 2. Tailor its questions to your purpose and audience.

Craft the document's contents for quick comprehension and ready use. Do not include everything you know; include only what the user needs and what the purpose requires. (You can provide more information later, if necessary.)

Choose the right presentation medium. If you are representing an organization, use its template (if it has one) for briefing memos. Communicate your memo or statement on the organization's letterhead stationary. If you are free to design the communication, fit it into one or two well-designed pages, as described earlier in this chapter. If the situation demands, you might also use a cover letter or attachments. Note: Before attaching anything crucial, consider the circumstances of reception, or how the document will be read and used. Attachments sometimes get detached when the document is circulated.

After drafting the communication, review and revise as needed (Checklists, chapter 2). If you are pressed for time, revise only the overview to focus the message sharply. From the reader's perspective, that is most important.

## Examples

These briefing memos by active citizens communicate opinion to local policy makers by e-mail, more or less effectively.

*Example 1*

## Scenario

Local government officials anticipate a farmer's request to operate a concentrated animal feeding operation (CAFO) in the municipality. It will be the first request of its type made since the municipality adopted a comprehensive plan for land use and a zoning ordinance. In that ordinance, although it is ambiguous, CAFOs may be considered as conditional uses of agricultural land to be permitted only if they meet site-specific conditions.

In preparation for reviewing the anticipated request and making a decision, the municipal official who chairs the planning commission begins to self-educate regarding CAFOs. His first objective is to become familiar with state law governing local authority to regulate CAFOs. He browses county and state government listservs; identifies technical and legal experts for possible consultation; attends relevant workshops, public hearings, and meetings; searches databases maintained by the state association of municipal officers and state government agencies; and searches municipal archives of public comment during the process of zoning adoption.

In a public meeting, he offers a preliminary interpretation of state law setting boundaries on municipal authority regarding CAFOs. A resident attending the meeting questions his interpretation. After the meeting, she offers to research the matter further. Given his lack of staff and the limited time he can devote to any single problem, he accepts her offer.

She locates the relevant state law and regulations online and reads them. She telephones state officials involved in authoring and implementing the regulations to ask about interpretations. They refer her to current case law on CAFOs and municipalities. Following up on their referrals and using the help of librarians in the state law school, she reads synopses of relevant current and pending cases.

Several days after the meeting in which she raised questions, she composes a one-page summary of findings and includes her interpretation of them. She e-mails the summary to the local official.

The sample briefing memo that follows was attached to an e-mail message.

## E-MAIL MESSAGE

Doug,

I recognize that the township supervisors and planning commissioners are trying to operate within state law on CAFOs. It's a complicated task, and I appreciate the careful thought you are putting into it. My intention is to help by getting good advice on interpreting state regulations so that we rightly know what authority Gregg Township has regarding CAFOs.

You raised two concerns in the July meeting of township supervisors. In the attached memo, I report what I've found and what I think regarding those two concerns. Basically, I find and I believe that the township has the necessary standing and authority to regulate CAFOs. You might want to talk to Douglas Goodlander (my source in Harrisburg). I'll call you later this week to see if you want to talk about any of this.

Catherine

## ATTACHMENT

### Memorandum

#### *Summary*

Gregg Township has "zoned in" the possibility of CAFOs, and it may regulate them within the limits of state law.

#### *The Prohibition of CAFOs*

You say, "You can't zone concentrated animal feeding operations out [prohibit them by means of zoning]." *Reference:* Pennsylvania State Association of Township Supervisors. See July issue of *PA Township News* for article "Avoiding Controversy: How Townships Can Minimize Conflicts between Residents and Intensive Ag Operations."

I say: Gregg has provided for the possibility of CAFOs operating in the township by making "feedlots" a conditional use in the agriculture zone. If "feedlots" can be construed to include CAFOs, then Gregg has "zoned in" the possibility. The zoning ordinance has a procedure for permitting, or not permitting, conditional uses based on case-by-case review for specified criteria. *Source:* Gregg Township Zoning Ordinance, Article 3, Agricultural Zone, Conditional Uses, C.4 Feedlots (p. 10), and Article 9, Conditional Uses, C. Criteria (pp. 3–4).

### Municipal Regulation of CAFOs

You say, "I read the state regulation as taking the wind out of our sails in regulating CAFOs." *Reference:* The "pre-emption of local ordinances" provision of the Rules and Regulations, 25 PA Chapter 83 Subchapter D, 803.25 (b) for the Nutrient Management Act (3 P.S.1701 et seq.) published in the *Pennsylvania Bulletin,* Vol. 27, No. 26, June 28, 1997.

I say: municipalities can regulate CAFOs. The next section of 83.205 (part c) states that "nothing in this act or this subchapter prevents a municipality from adopting and enforcing ordinances or regulations that are consistent with/no more stringent than the state act." Beyond nutrient management [antipollution measures to prevent excess nutrients in animal manure from entering water sources], other issues presented by CAFOs such as odor, noise, air pollution, and road use can be locally regulated. *Source:* Douglas Goodlander of the Pennsylvania Conservation Commission. Goodlander is an author of 25 PA [nutrient management regulations] who has been involved in CAFO court cases in PA. He cautions that he can provide interpretation but not legal counsel. He encourages you to call him if you want (telephone number provided).

---

►— **WHAT EXAMPLE 1 SHOWS.** Two characteristics of this communication are especially noteworthy: its form and its intelligibility in context. Internet communications such as e-mail differ in several ways from other written or spoken communications. E-mail is typically more informal and personal and often has less regard for spelling or grammatical correctness. In a public process, if taken out of its original context, e-mail might embarrass the sender or recipient. Or it might compromise the action.

The intelligibility of this message relies on context. The sender and receiver know each other and have worked together before. They generally agree on the importance of local control in governance, but they might disagree on regulation of CAFOs. In the limited context of a policy process underway, they have been meeting and talking about this particular issue before this e-mail was sent. When the e-mail and its attachment are read together, they can be accurately understood in context. If they are read outside the context or if the two documents are separated and one is read without the other, the communication might be misinterpreted.

Why does this matter? Correspondence with an elected official is open to public scrutiny. In addition, the e-mail and its attached memo will become part of a permanent public record. The elected official in this example is obliged to archive all communications on public matters and to make them available to anyone with a right to public information now or in the future. You may have seen caution-ary evidence, such as the following notification at the end of a town officer's e-mail:

> Pursuant to North Carolina General Statutes Chapter 132, Public Records, this electronic mail message and any attach-ments hereto, as well as any electronic mail message(s) that may be sent in response to it, may be considered public record and as such are subject to request and review by anyone at any time.

Context affects intelligibility in another way, too. If the two parts of the communication, the e-mail and its attachment, become sepa-rated in a process of referring or forwarding the documents, the tone of either one might lead to misinterpretation. The brisk tone of the memo might seem unfriendly. (Method, chapter 2, advises you to consider the attitude a communication conveys.) Contrasting view-points are summarized in efficient parallelism ("You say, I say"). Only necessary words are used. Citations and contact information are stra-tegically included to save time for a busy official who does much of his own research. There is a downside to this efficiency, however. While its intention might be to help, the briefing memo's terse style lacks the sympathetic tone of the covering e-mail that acknowledges the difficult problem the official must resolve. If the two documents are received separately, the reader's reception of either might be affected.

Communication is more than an information exchange; it is also a social interaction. The tone or implied attitude of a policy commu-nication can affect its reception and possibly a working relationship. Recalling that policy makers receive lots of unsolicited communica-tions, you should be aware that tone explains why some communi-cations are ignored. Memos or statements that are expressly hostile or that seem closed-minded are not likely to be read, to receive a response, or to be useful to the process.

### Example 2

Here are several more communications that illustrate good tone and bad tone in statements of opinion. Citizens e-mailed these messages to an elected official in county government regarding a proposed merger of city and county schools.

**Good tone**. The following three opinion statements got the policy maker's careful attention and received a substantive reply.

A. You currently face a difficult decision regarding the proposed merger of [Town and County] Schools. I am writing to suggest a public referendum on this matter given the significant impact that the results of your decision will have on your constituency. Thanks for taking time to consider this request.

B. The merger discussion is heating up quickly, and I'm hoping the real issue of the disparate funding for the two systems doesn't get lost in the commotion. The push for a referendum, called for by so many [Town] parents, seems a veiled attempt to simply stifle discussion, allowing the real issue to again get swept under the rug, still unfixed.

C. Here are a few questions I'd love to have answered. I know you're busy and probably receiving hundreds (??!!) of emails daily on this issue. I hope you can fit me in.

1. Do you see a funding imbalance between the two systems?
   ...
   We need a solution. Thank you for considering my questions.

**Bad tone**. In contrast, the following three opinion statements (like many similar ones generated by a letter-writing campaign) got little attention and received no reply.

A. I understand that the [County] Board of Commissioners is evaluating a merger of the [Town and County] School Systems. I would like to communicate that:

- I, along with most of my local colleagues and neighbors, are vehemently OPPOSED to a merger.

- I request that a public REFERENDUM be held on this issue ASAP.

- Unless proper procedure is followed throughout, a proposed merger will be challenged in the [State] and Federal courts to the extent necessary.

- The voting records of the entire board will be well remembered and publicized in time for the next ELECTION.

B. I am greatly disappointed in your decision Wednesday night to short circuit democracy in our county. None of you ran last November with a position on school merger. You have suddenly sprung it on the citizens of the county. Since you would not face voters on the issue, you should allow a referendum on the issue in the county. Otherwise, you should delay the issue until an election year, and run on your beliefs. The idea that you can have a "stealth" merger of school systems and avoid the will of the citizens of the county, as some of you seem to believe, is not in keeping with the traditions of transparency and progressive politics in our county. I voted for you all last November. But I did not vote for school merger. Now I feel that your election was as much a sham. I would like a chance to vote on school merger or to vote again on your positions on the county commission.

C. I am very concerned about an article in the *Herald* which indicates that the schools in [County and Town] may merge. I don't understand what the advantage of such a move would be. If there is an advantage to the move please let me know what it is. If there is no advantage to the move, please let me know by ignoring this message.

━━━━━━━━

➤ **WHAT EXAMPLE 2 SHOWS.** These examples teach communicators to make careful choices. A public policy communicator has to make many competing choices. Purpose, contents, presentation style and tone, medium of delivery, and concern for immediate reception and use as well as the permanent record—all these must be considered and choices made. The choices are important because the consequences are significant. The outcomes of policy affect real people and places.

## Summary and Preview

Information for a purpose and for targeted readers is characteristic in policy work. Opinion and information are vital to the process. This chapter focuses on two common ways of informing policy makers in a pointed manner. A briefing memo is the written equivalent of the spoken one-minute "elevator speech" or the one-minute oral summary of testimony. A statement of personal opinion is the equivalent of a voicemail message. Keep the tone of such communications professional and friendly, or at least neutral. Politeness is highly valued in the cultural context of public policy making.

In chapter 9, next, you'll learn about another way of informing policy makers that allows extensive interaction, testifying as a witness in public hearings.

# Testimony: Witness in a Public Hearing

## Key Concepts

- prepare to write and to speak
- prepare to present an oral statement and to answer questions

Policy makers and administrators are required to deliberate publicly and to seek input. Witnesses provide input. This chapter prepares you to testify as a witness in a governmental public hearing.

In the U.S. federal government, "sunshine" or public access laws mandate open hearings for all legislative functions—making law, appropriating funds, overseeing government operations, investigating abuse or wrongdoing, and approving nominations or appointments to office. Hearings are held in executive and legislative branches of federal government. In state and local governments, public deliberation is mandated, but formal hearings are not as commonly held as at the federal level.

In government organized by a political party structure, the majority party (the party in power) chairs committees and thus sets the agenda for committee work, including public hearings. Committee chairs (with their staffs) decide whether to hold a hearing on a topic within their jurisdiction, what the purpose of a hearing will be, and who will be on the witness list. Topics and purposes of hearings reflect the committee's jurisdiction and the chair's political agenda. The agenda might or might not reflect cooperation between the majority and minority interests of members on the committee.

Several committees might hold hearings on different aspects of the same topic, especially if the topic concerns a hot issue that crosses jurisdictions. Hot issues are those that are currently in the news, controversial, or especially significant in some way. Most hearings are not about hot issues, however. Most hearings are workaday sessions to oversee government operations, to decide on appropriations of funds, to reauthorize programs, and so forth. They do the routine work of governance.

Public affairs television usually does not broadcast these routine hearings. Selected daily hearings are summarized on the government page of newspapers and some advocacy group websites. Some congressional committee websites broadcast hearings in progress.

In the executive branch, departments or agencies hold public hearings on issues within their regulatory responsibility. Some are held in the field, in geographic areas or political districts directly affected. Executive branch hearings vary in format from informal public meetings to formal deliberative sessions. The state environmental agency's hearing on water protection described in Example 2, later in this chapter, illustrates informal field hearings in which executives, staff, and witnesses freely discuss a topic.

Taking U.S. congressional committee hearings as the model, hearings typically follow this order of events. After the chair opens the hearing, announces the purpose, and states his or her position on the topic, the committee members then state their positions and, possibly, their constituency's concerns regarding the topic. Next, invited witnesses testify on the topic. Following the testimonies, the usual practice is for committee members to question the witnesses.

In principle, anyone might be invited to testify who can provide information that lawmakers or administrators seek. In reality, witnesses testify at the federal level only by request of the committee. At state and local levels, the witness list is more open. There, you may be invited, or you may ask, to testify. If you wish to testify, you contact the staff of the committee or the agency holding the hearing.

In the communication situation of a typical hearing, witnesses testify as spokespersons for an organization or a government agency.

Occasionally, individual citizens testify on their own or their community's behalf. Witnesses must relate their special concerns to a policy context and their agendas to other agendas. Policy makers and witnesses interact face-to-face, and exchanges might be polite or confrontational. Questioning might be focused or loose. Questioning is always political, and sometimes it is bluntly partisan. The atmosphere might be orderly or hectic. The time limits are always tight—typically one to five minutes for each witness to present testimony and five minutes for each member to question all the witnesses. There might be multiple rounds of questioning. Hearings can last for hours or days if the committee or the witness list is large.

Legislative hearings are characteristically more freeform than legal hearings in administration of justice. In legislative hearings, generally, there are no prescribed rules for disclosing evidence or for objecting to questions as there are in law court hearings. Exceptions are investigative hearings in which witnesses might testify under oath. Even then, questioning is not constrained by rules. Consequently, witnesses for legislative hearings must prepare well for anticipated and unanticipated developments in the question-and-answer session that follows presentation (Smith 1993).

Everything communicated in a hearing goes (via a legislative stenographer) into a transcript. This transcript is the official public record of the hearing. There are actually two public records, unofficial and official. Unofficially, the hearing might be broadcast and reported by news media followed by commentary in all media. These influential accounts shape public discourse and the perception of problems; however, they are not authoritative. They would not be included in a legislative history, for example. For the authoritative and official record of a hearing, a stenographer records the statements, questions, and answers verbatim, exactly as they are given. In current legislative reporting practice, the verbatim transcript cannot be edited, except to correct factual errors.

The transcript is later (sometimes months later) printed and published by the superintendent of government documents through the government printing office. This is the official, or legal, record of the hearing. Published hearing records are important for democratic self-governance because they give continuing public access over time to the accurate and full information produced by a hearing. That information is useful for many purposes. Journalists, law clerks, academic researchers in many fields, legislative staff, lobbyists, advocates, and active citizens use hearing transcripts as sources. Published hearings are primary sources for legislative history research, for example. They are also major sources for determining a law's original intent when the law is being adjudicated.

In the overall significance of government hearings for democracy, witness testimony is most important. For witnesses, it is an opportunity to bring concerns to the table, to talk directly with policy makers, to make personal or professional knowledge useful for solving problems. For policy makers, hearings offer a rare opportunity to talk directly with knowledgeable witnesses and to question them. Policy makers appreciate that interaction. Most information they receive is filtered through staff or advisors. They like having the chance to interact with other sources of information and perspective.

## How to Deliver Oral Testimony Based on a Written Statement

*Goal:* To speak authoritatively and to answer questions responsively in public deliberation.

*Objective:* Skill of writing speakable text, skill of speaking easily from written text, and readiness to answer anticipated and unanticipated questions.

*Scope:* Pinpointed topic pertinent to a hearing's purpose and the witness's role.

*Product:* Two expected communication products are as follows:

- short oral summary, either a list of talking points (outline for speaking) or a one-page overview (to be read aloud)
- full written statement, possibly with appendices, to be included in the record of the hearing

*Strategy:* Confident and useful public testimony resulting from advance preparation.

### Develop a Testimony in Context

Obviously, witnesses must know their subject and their message. More important, witnesses must understand the purpose(s) of the hearing and their own role and purpose(s) for testifying. Effective witnessing is achieved by presenting concisely and by responding credibly to questions. Responding to questions effectively is most important. If you are on the witness list, you are acknowledged as having something relevant to say. You do not need to impress people by showing how much you know about the topic. Focus strongly on your purpose and your message in relation to the hearing's purpose.

*Know the context.* To what policy process does the hearing relate? To what political agenda? Who's holding the hearing? What is the stated purpose of the hearing? What is the political purpose? Who else is on the witness list? What are their messages likely to be?

*Know your message.* Distill your message into one to two sentences that you can remember and can say easily. How does your message relate to the purpose of the hearing? How does it relate to other witnesses' messages? Anticipate committee members' responses and questions. What are you likely to be asked?

*Know your role.* Are you speaking for an organization? For yourself? Why are you testifying? What do the organizers of the hearing hope your testimony will accomplish?

*Know the communication situation.* Will the press attend the hearing? Are you available for interviews after the hearing? Will the hearing be televised? How is the hearing room arranged? Do the arrangements allow you to use the charts, posters, or slides? Are those visual aids a good idea if the room lights cannot be dimmed (due to televising of the hearing)? What is the location for the hearing? If you are using charts, posters, or slides, how will you transport them? Who will set them up in the hearing room?

*Rehearse your delivery.* Will you read your statement or say it? Generally, saying it is preferred. Be ready to do either, however. Rehearse by reading the full statement aloud and by speaking from an outline. You'll discover which way is easier for you and which you need to practice more.

## Task #1. Write the testimony

Use the Method (chapter 2) to plan testimony in both oral and written forms. Some witnesses prefer to outline the oral summary first and then to develop the full written statement from that outline. Others prefer the opposite way. They write the full statement first; then they outline an oral summary based on the written statement.

The key to both? *Preparation.* Write out your oral summary, even if it is simply a list of talking points on an index card. The written list will provide confidence and control as you testify. Recall that everything said in a governmental public hearing is recorded and that the record is made publicly available. Do not plan to wing it or to testify extemporaneously. If you do that, you risk exceeding time limits, which committee chairs do not like. And you might forget important information, say more or less than you intend to have on the public record, or find yourself being asked questions (about something you said) that you are not prepared to answer.

If you are free to organize your testimony, you might want to use the following template. Use it in outline form for the oral summary, and expand it appropriately for the full written statement. Put extensive support in appendices, not in the main statement. (Both the oral and written versions will be included in the transcript of the hearing.) Here is the template:

- title page or header to identify the organization and the witness, the agency holding the hearing, the topic, the date, and the location of the hearing
- greeting to thank the organizers for the opportunity to testify and to state why the topic is important to the witness
- message to state the main information the testimony provides
- support (evidence, grounds) for the message
- relevance of the message to the hearing's purpose
- optional: discussion or background to add perspective on the message (only if relevant or if specifically requested by conveners of the hearing)
- closing to conclude the testimony and invite questions

### Task #2. Write the full statement

The written statement might use the same organization as the oral summary. The written statement may be longer, include more details, and be accompanied by appendices. It can be any length, but it should be no longer than necessary. Even if the written statement is lengthy, it must be organized and concise. That way, it is more likely to be read and used. Tip: good organization enables you to condense on demand if, for example, you are asked by the committee chair to limit your remarks. If that happens, present your message, state its relevance to the hearing's purpose, and conclude by saying that you will be glad to answer questions. Add omitted content in your answers to questions.

## Task #3. Present the testimony

The following tips are important.

- Summarize. During oral delivery, whether reading a document aloud or speaking from an outline, state only the essentials. Save the details for the question-and-answer period.

- State the message early and emphatically. Whether reading a text or speaking from an outline, state the message up front.

- Stay within time limits. Usually, the chair of a hearing will tell you the time limits. If not, assume that you have two to five minutes for a summary. Do not go over the limit.

- Listen. Closely attend to the opening statements by the committee chair and the committee members. Opening statements cue the questions that you might be asked. Or they might include content to which you want to respond later, when it is your turn to speak. Listen also to other testimonies. Committee members might ask you to comment on other witnesses' testimonies.

- Answer credibly. The question-and-answer time is often the most important part of a hearing. Committee members and witnesses alike agree on this. For committee members, it is a chance to interact directly with knowledgeable people. Members usually ask prepared questions to get important concerns, as well as witnesses' responses to the concerns, on the record. For witnesses, the question-and-answer time is a chance to connect their message to varied agendas represented in the questions or to pinpoint the usefulness of their knowledge to the committee. Witness effectiveness depends primarily on the witness's credible (honest, accurately informed, relevant) responsiveness to questioning.

After you have presented your testimony statement, shift your attention to question-and-answer communication. Follow these important guidelines:

- Listen to the questions asked of other witnesses. Do not daydream or otherwise lose focus while others are being questioned.

- Make sure you hear each question correctly when you are being questioned. If you are not sure you heard the question correctly, ask to have it repeated.

- Answer the question that is asked, not some other question that you half-heard or that you prefer.

- Stop when you have answered a question. Wait for a follow-up question. Postpone details, elaboration, or qualification on your original answer until a follow-up question allows you to provide them.

- Do not lie or invent information. If you hear yourself fabricating an answer (perhaps out of nervousness), stop. Politely ask to have your answer removed from the record, and begin again.

- Handle these situations especially carefully:

  - You are asked for your personal opinion. When you testify as spokesperson for an organization, be careful to present the organization's viewpoint. Avoid giving a personal opinion unless specifically requested, and then only if you appropriately can do so. If you do, be careful to distinguish your own view from the organization's.

  - You don't know the answer. Depending on the dynamics at the moment (neutral or friendly or confrontational) and considering the effect on your credibility of not answering, you might choose among these options: Simply say you do not know, say you are not prepared to answer but can provide the answer later, ask if you might restate the question in a different way that you can better answer, or defer to another witness who can better answer the question.

  - Your credentials are challenged, or your credibility is attacked. Do not get angry. Do not confront the challenger or attacker. Politely state your or your organization's qualifications to speak on the topic of the hearing. Restate why you are testifying or why the hearing topic is important to you or your organization. Maintain your role in the hearing as a source of information and perspective not offered by others. Maintain your composure.

## Two Examples with Scenarios

Many excellent samples of written testimony can be found on the websites of respected nonprofit advocacy organizations, public policy institutes, and some government agencies. For example, see the following:

- Human Rights Watch http://www.hrw.org/en/search/apachesolr_ search/congressional+testimony
- Cato Institute http://www.cato.org/pubs/pubs.html
- U.S. Government Accountability Office Reports and Testimonies http://www.gao.gov

Example 1 on military health care benefits was written by the professional in federal government shown previously (Example 1, chapter 3; Example 4, chapter 7). She wrote the statement for presentation by another witness. Example 2 was written and presented by the citizen participating in local government shown previously (Example 1, chapter 8). Scenarios remind you of the contexts for these testimony statements.

*Example 1*

## Scenario

The Office of the Chief Surgeon, Reserve Armed Forces, is asked by interested congressional offices to justify the request for increased health care benefits for Reserve Component Soldiers. The House Armed Services Committee asks for a witness to testify in an upcoming hearing, specifically to justify increased dental care benefits. Senior officers are unavailable to write the testimony. The Chief of Patient Information is asked to draft a statement making the case for more dental care. A senior officer will orally deliver the testimony as witness. Delegation of writing or "ghost-writing" is characteristic in her workplace, as in others. The work of many professionals may be present, unidentified, in a document that carries only the organization's name and perhaps the name of the head administrator.

This action officer has not previously written congressional testimony. She is uncertain about the genre. Also, she does not know the committee's political agenda and related purpose for this hearing. She has little experience in writing for congressional audiences. She has not attended a hearing. There are no guidelines for writing congressional testimony and there is no template for a witness statement in the Army manual of procedure or style. As an astute professional communicator, however, she knows that context or genre, purpose, and audience are as important as message. So, despite a hectic schedule, she makes the time to prepare for writing. She consults textbooks on policy writing and government writing. She searches the Internet for samples of testimony by government witnesses. Reading actual samples gives her a feel for the expected form. Asking experienced peers about the committee gives her a sense of the context. She drafts a statement, and circulates it in her office for specialist review of content. She also sends it to a friend in another office, an experienced staff member for a senator who serves on relevant committees. The friend provides informal contextual review. Once formal review by staff is completed, the document comes back to the action officer. She makes all changes, then she gives the document to the senior officer who will be the witness. He reviews and requests changes, which she makes. She briefs the witness on the testimony's topic. Before the committee hearing date, a "mock" hearing will be held involving key participants from all agencies who reviewed the statement.

Unclassified
Statement by Colonel Michael Flynn
Chief Surgeon of the Reserve Armed Forces of America
Before the House Armed Services Committee
Subcommittee on Oversight and Investigation
Second Session, 110th Congress
on
Dental Readiness in the Reserve Armed Forces of America

May 17, 2008

Chairman Smith, Ranking Member Clay, as the Chief Surgeon of the Reserve Armed Forces of America, I am here today to answer your concerns about the dental readiness of the Soldiers in the Reserve Armed Forces of America.

The interest of the subcommittee on this issue is well placed. Dental readiness of our Citizen-Soldiers is a critical element in their capability to meet Department of Defense requirements for deployment.

## Current Situation

The transition from a Strategic Reserve to an Operational Force has placed tremendous strain on the Reserve Armed Forces of America. Historically, as a strategic reserve, Soldiers and leaders of the Reserve Armed Forces addressed dental readiness issues at the mobilization station. The implementation of the Department of Defense's twelve month mobilization policy in February 2007 forced units to address dental readiness at home station in order to maximize collective training at the mobilization station.

The Reserve Armed Forces Medical Team, in conjunction with our Armed Forces Dental Command partners, has successfully managed this transition to an Operational Force. Since the beginning of the fiscal year, our units have prepared seven Brigade Combat Units (BCUs) for deployment, with each unit sending their units to the mobilization station over 90% dentally ready. These incredible readiness rates are a tremendous improvement over their previous mobilizations in 2003, when the average dental readiness rate was 13%. This significant decrease in the number of training days lost to dental treatment at mobilization station has enabled commanders to focus on collective training and maximize boots-on-ground time in theater.

Due to the low level of baseline dental readiness in the Reserve Armed Forces—currently only 40% of the force is dentally ready to deploy—truly herculean efforts must be applied by our units once a unit is alerted. Dental activities compete for the time of leaders, Soldiers, and families as a unit prepares to go to war. Soldiers that are cross-leveled to a ready unit dilute that unit's readiness and lengthen training timelines.

In order to improve the baseline readiness of the Reserve Armed Forces, the same programs, policies, and procedures that have been used to successfully prepare these BCUs need to be applied to our force as a whole.

## Actions Taken

The Reserve Armed Forces, in conjunction with the Office of the Surgeon General and the Armed Forces Dental Command, has developed a multifaceted plan that has been approved by both the Army and Reserve Armed Forces leadership.

The cornerstone of this plan is the ability to provide dental treatment to our Soldiers outside of alert.

...

The Armed Forces Selected Reserve Dental Readiness Program (SRDRP) will enable units to provide dental treatment to soldiers through local contracts or utilizing the Reserve Health Readiness Program (RHRP).

The Reserve Armed Forces is a true reflection of our nation, and very few of our Citizen-Soldiers have private dental insurance. The participation rate in the TRICARE Reserve Dental Program has hit a plateau at 8%. The ability to provide treatment to our soldiers through the Armed Forces Selected Reserve Dental Readiness Program will have a tremendous impact on the readiness of the Reserve Armed Forces.

This program will also enable the Reserve Armed Forces to maximize the benefits of the Armed Forces Dental Command's initiatives.

...

With treatment programs in place, we must also address barriers to compliance with readiness requirements. Active component soldiers do not take unpaid leave to go to the dentist, nor should a Reserve Armed Forces soldier. The ability to provide two medical readiness days per soldier would be a powerful incentive for the soldier to complete readiness requirements, as well as a tool for our commanders to ensure compliance.

...

In addition to treatment and incentives, there must be enforcement as recommended by the Commission on Reserve Affairs. As alerted units prepare to go overseas, dental readiness is consistently the main reason for soldier ineligibility for deployment. The Armed Forces have multiple systems which provide unit and senior leaders the capability to track a unit's progress as they prepare for deployment....These tools must be applied and dental readiness enforced by leaders at all levels throughout the Reserve Armed Forces to improve the readiness of our soldiers.

Lastly, in order to execute these programs and sustain an increase in the dental readiness of the Reserve Armed Forces, we must have the appropriate staffing. The Reserve Armed Forces dental corps is currently less than 70% strength, and the majority of remaining providers are eligible for retirement. This committee is considering the Department of Defense's request to increase the retirement age of Reserve Armed Forces healthcare providers from age 65 to age 69.

This would create the same standard for all three components of service. I would ask that this committee support that request and make that adjustment to the law.

...

Likewise, as a reserve component consisting largely of part-time warriors, the Reserve Armed Forces relies heavily on its cadre of full-time personnel to do the administration, maintenance, and training preparation required to produce a ready force. The president's budget request currently before Congress seeks an increase in the level of full-time manning in our force. This is critical. We urge Congress to support this increase.

### Conclusion

This is a very exciting time to be in the Reserve Armed Forces. We have deployed over 300,000 dentally ready soldiers in support of the nation since September 11th 2001. Even so, we can do better. The Army and the Reserve Armed Forces are committed to our Citizen-Soldiers, by caring for them and improving their dental readiness.

I am grateful for this opportunity to appear before this subcommittee and look forward to answering your questions.

---

**➤ WHAT THIS EXAMPLE SHOWS.** The testimony writer's consideration of semantics, or word meanings, is noteworthy. Sensitivity to politics surrounding Reserve Armed Forces health care in general, and dental care in particular, is shown here by careful word choice, such as "dental readiness" and "successfully managed transition" and "tremendous improvement." These wordings characterize achievement under difficult working conditions. Careful choice of organization is also evident. The testimony is organized narratively to tell a story of good management in a trying situation. These presentation techniques, deliberate word choice and storytelling, are not deceptive. They are not "spin." Rather, they are ethical (accurate, demonstrable) and rhetorically effective (credible) ways to characterize the organization's definition of the problem and message. Implicit meaning supports explicit statement well. The example illustrates an aspect of policy writing not noted in previous commentary on other samples, care for the meaningful interpretation of policy information. The language used to characterize a problem influences (Bardach 2011). A story about the problem informs (Stone 2002).

### *Example 2*

---

**Scenario**

---

A resident of a rural area known for the high quality of its cold-water fishing streams serves as a board member of a local conservation group. She learns of proposed changes in state policy for classifying waterways according to their quality. Four regional field hearings will be held to hear public comment on the agency's draft of a revised guidance manual for implementation of state water-quality regulations.

With the help of the state agency's staff, the resident obtains copies of the old and the new guidance manual, and she carefully reads the proposed changes. In her judgment, the new guidance draft weakens the standards. She alerts the local conservation group for which she is a board member. She asks the board to authorize her as spokesperson for the group in the upcoming hearings, and they do so. She writes testimony stating the position. She telephones the agency staff and asks to testify. In the call, she provides her credentials and says whom she represents. The staff member who is organizing the field hearings puts her on the schedule of witnesses.

In the hearing, she testifies with other witnesses from throughout her region. All witnesses provide a written copy of their testimony for the public record of the hearing. Following the testimonies, witnesses are encouraged to question the agency's managers. This reverses the usual question-and-answer procedure. Normally, conveners of a hearing question the witnesses. On this occasion, however, the agency managers want to demonstrate more than usual responsiveness to public comment.

---

Shown here is the written statement for the record (edited to reduce length). An oral summary was delivered.

### Living with Exceptional Value

Testimony by the Penns Valley Conservation Association (PVCA)

Public Hearing on Anti-Degradation Implementation Pennsylvania Department of Environmental Protection (PA-DEP) Bureau of Water Quality and Wastewater Management, Harrisburg, PA, August 1, 2001.

Thank you for providing us the opportunity to comment on DEP's draft Guidance for water quality protection. We strongly support DEP's anti-degradation program. Because we support it, we are concerned about how local communities such as ours perceive and participate in the program. We focus our testimony on the need to make implementation more inclusive and to ensure public participation. We offer related suggestions for revising the draft Guidance.

Our message to DEP is this: The goal of regulation is water quality protection. To the extent possible under Pennsylvania law, DEP's guidance should assume that implementation requires equal participation by petitioners or applicants and by communities that must live with the consequences of permitted or approved activity. The Department's function is to arbitrate between these parties and their interests while protecting the larger public interest. Petitioners and applicants are well prepared to present their legitimate interests and the commercial value of granting their request. Communities are less prepared to protect their interests. To carry out its function, DEP must ensure effective public participation.

Addressing those concerns one at a time, and relating them to the draft Guidance:

- *The goal of the program is water quality protection.* The draft Guidance does not make sufficiently clear that the purpose of the anti-degradation program is to *protect* all surface waters from adverse impacts on fish species, flora, and fauna by activities receiving a DEP permit or approval. True, policy is stated in chapter 1 and regulations as well as standards are identified at the start of chapter 2. But discussion sections throughout the draft create doubt that DEP will protect Pennsylvania's resources as required by regulation and federal law.

  ...

- *Guidance should assume that protection requires full participation of affected communities in addition to applicants or petitioners. DEP's function is to arbitrate between those interests and to protect the larger public interest.* The draft Guidance focuses exclusively on DEP's response to applicants or petitioners for permits or approvals. Community representatives such as citizens' groups must also be recognized as key participants in permitting or approval processes. The public will refer to the Guidance for policies, definitions, and procedures. The Guidance might function as the procedures manual for public participation, but the current draft does not serve that function well.

  . . .

- *To carry out its function, DEP needs effective public participation.* According to the Guidance, applicants or petitioners are encouraged to go beyond public notification to seek public input. That is not enough. The Department itself should actively seek and inform community input. On that topic, we must caution DEP about an effort, noted in chapter 4, on the processing of petitions, evaluations, and assessments to change a designated use. We are concerned about the pilot program of notifying landowners who border streams or stream segments being considered for HQ or EV status. That notification is dangerously insufficient. To notify landowners alone—and not local conservation groups, watershed associations, or municipal planning commissions—favors one constituency, property owners. Worse, to notify landowners without spelling out which activities or permits might affect a protected stream is likely to generate misinformed reaction. Backlash against protection is fueled by selective and cryptic public notification.

To summarize, experience teaches our organization that classifying a stream as High Quality or Exceptional Value is relatively easy. But implementation of protection on the ground in the community can be hard. We've identified three main obstacles: public ignorance or misunderstanding of the anti-degradation program's purpose and methods, burdensome permitting, and weak coordination among DEP bureaus sharing responsibility for water quality protection.

I will briefly describe our experience in attempting to protect special waters and a watershed. Direct practical experience is the context for our testimony.

. . .

## Conclusion

PVCA applauds the new ground the DEP is exploring in financing watershed assessment and restoration activities by local communities through its Growing Greener program. Conservation groups like the PVCA are adopting watershed-wide approaches to restoration, while monitoring local activities for adverse effects on watersheds. We would like to see watershed concepts reflected in DEP's regulatory and permitting process. We would like support for comprehensive restoration efforts. And, we would like to see stronger intergovernmental coordination in protecting special waters.

This concludes our testimony. We refer you to our accompanying chapter-by-chapter list of suggested revisions to the draft Guidance. We are glad to answer questions now.

---

•—• **WHAT THIS EXAMPLE SHOWS.** This written statement is organized to support spoken delivery under variable time limits. (Sometimes a witness is given more or less time than expected for presentation.) The introduction and summary can be presented in one minute. The introduction, summary, and list of concerns (without details beyond the first sentence in each section) can be presented in two to three minutes. The whole can be presented in five to seven minutes (Task 1). However, individual sentences are too long for easy speaking and listening. Tighter sentence structure could make the statement easier to say and to hear.

Together, these examples illustrate the two halves of public hearing testimony. Example 1 on military dental readiness illustrates the oral summary, while Example 2 on stream classification illustrates the written statement for the record. This combination serves the dual purposes of face-to-face discussion and on-the-record accountability.

## Summary and Preview

Testimony in a public hearing is a highly visible way of getting your knowledge and perspective into the public record. Chapter 10, next, introduces an equally important, less visible way of influencing policy, providing public comment on proposed administrative action.

## References

Bardach, E. 2011. Semantic tips: A summary. *A practical guide for policy analysis: The eightfold path to more effective problem solving*, Appendix C. 4th ed. Washington, DC: CQ Press.

Smith, Catherine F. 1993. "Is it worth fixing this plane?" The rhetorical life of information in a congressional oversight hearing on the B-1 bomber. *Studies in technical communication: Selected papers of the 1992 CCCC and NCTE conferences*, pp. 111–46. Ed. Brenda Sims. Denton: University of North Texas Press.

Stone, D. 2002. Symbols. In *Policy paradox: The art of political decision making*. Rev. ed., pp. 137–62. New York: W.W. Norton.

✦◦

# CHAPTER 10

# Written Public Comment: Influence Administration

## Key Concept

- public input on rule making

Too few people take advantage of an opportunity to set the standards and write the rules by which law is administered and enforced. When a government agency seeks public comment on proposed regulation, your response might make a difference. This chapter shows you how to write a formal public comment in rule making and adjudication procedures.

In federal government, after a law is enacted, an executive branch agency begins rule making to implement the law. This involves developing standards and regulations for administering and enforcing the law. As required by the Administrative Procedures Act as well as other laws and executive orders, the agency must seek public comment on the proposed standards and regulations before they can be put in force. Sometimes, oral hearings are held; typically, written comments are requested.

While federal agencies are required to seek public comment, they have discretion regarding the use of comments received. In federal and many states' rule making procedures, agencies may choose or choose not to describe whether and how they modified the proposed regulation in response to the comments received. For example, in the milk labeling case (chapter 1) the Bureau of Food Safety and Laboratory Services of the Pennsylvania Department of Agriculture (PDA) described a modification this way:

191

PDA has received a great deal of input on the standards set forth in [the new standard on milk labeling announced on October 24, 2007] and previously decided to inform you on November 21, 2007 that certain deadlines stated in that document were being changed from January 1, 2008 to February 1, 2008. We are now in a position to inform you further as to the results of reviewing the input we received. Enclosed please find a new document titled "Revised Standards and Procedures for the Approval of Proposed Labeling of Fluid Milk" dated January 17, 2008.... Please review this document carefully and govern yourself accordingly.

In state and local governments, public comment is not sought as routinely as in federal government. However, states must seek public comment in regulatory procedures for granting, revoking, or renewing permits for activities that affect public life.

Regrettably, few citizens know about this opportunity to provide input, and few engage it. As a result, narrowly interested groups dominate the rule making process. Broader participation is needed.

Federal, state, and local agencies welcome any type of comment that can help them make and justify their decisions. The comment might be a technical analysis, a philosophical argument, an opinion based on personal experience, advocacy, or a request to hold a public meeting on the proposed action. Responsible agencies review all written comments. They take seriously well-prepared comments that suggest realistic and feasible alternatives.

Public comment is important because public policy broadly affects present and future life. A call for public comment invites any member of the public—individuals, communities, organizations—to influence the standards and regulations that affect real lives, livelihoods, and environments. Public comment is easy to make. Anybody can write a useful comment. The more who do so, the better the likelihood of good government.

## How to Write a Public Comment

*Goal:* Knowledge of administrative procedures for implementing law, including the public's role in implementation.

*Objective:* To influence the administration of a law by contributing information relevant to standard setting, rule making, or permitting.

*Product:* Formal written comment.

*Scope:* Limited to the specific proposed administrative action.

*Strategy:* Base comments on your authority to respond, whether based on personal experience, organizational advocacy, vocational or professional background, or specialized knowledge.

While expert commentary is always appropriate, you need not be an expert to comment. Administrators want and need to hear from anyone who can make a useful comment. There is no template for public comments, unlike legal briefs. A simple letter can have an impact. If friends or a community organization shares your views, you might want to present a collective comment. You might sign for the group, or all individuals involved might sign, or the organization's officers might sign.

## Task #1. Find Calls for Public Comment

The U.S. government's official source for notifications of proposed rule making is the *Federal Register,* published daily. You can find the *Federal Register* either in government information depository libraries or online at http://www.gpo.gov/fdsysinfo/aboutfdsys.htm.

You will find calls for comment in the section titled "Proposed Rules" or the section titled "Notices." Look for announcements by agencies authorized to act on topics of concern to you.

Alternatively, if you already know the executive branch department, and within it the relevant agency that administers laws in your area of concern, do not go initially to the *Register.* It can be overwhelming, and you might have to look at the index every day to follow the government's activities on an issue of concern. Instead, first try the website of the relevant department (the Department of Transportation, for instance); search there for the relevant agency (National Highway Traffic Safety Administration, for instance). If you do not know what department or agency to search for, go to the website of an advocacy group associated with your concern. Browsing there is likely to turn up the name of both the department and agency. Then proceed with searching the agency's website for notifications.

If you are concerned about a state issue, you can find calls for public comment in state notifications, such as the *Pennsylvania Bulletin* or the *New York State Register.* Every state has one.

Familiarize yourself with the index and other finding aids for the state publication you are likely to use often.

Alternatively, if you know the jurisdiction for your concern, go first to the website of the state agency with jurisdiction. Or go to the websites of interested associations and advocacy groups to find where you can make a comment on an active issue.

If you want to comment on a local government matter, consult local newspapers. Local government calls for public comment are published in the public notices section of newspapers. Notifications are also posted in local government offices or, possibly, on their websites.

## Task #2. Write the Public Comment Document

In most respects, writing a public comment is like writing any other policy document. The demands for preparation and planning are the same. The same criteria for clarity, credibility, and conciseness apply. One possible difference: some calls for public input specify the exact information needed. If the call to which you are responding does specify the contents, provide them as requested. If you have additional information, include it too, but not at the expense of requested contents.

To help ensure that your comment will be taken seriously, include the following features and qualities:

- narrow focus
- evidence, analyses, and references supporting your view
- indication of public support of your view
- positive and feasible alternatives

Before you write, use the Method (chapter 2) to plan. After you write, check the product against the expected standards (Checklists, chapter 2).

# Four Examples with Scenarios

Examples here show administrative policy making. Examples 1 and 4 illustrate rule making by federal agencies, while Examples 2 and 3 illustrate adjudicative procedure by a state agency. Comment by experts, by nonprofit organizations, and by a civic group is shown. Scenarios provide context for each example.

*Example 1*

---

### Scenario

A national transportation safety investigative board holds four days of hearings on air bag safety. The board, which reports both to the Congress and to the executive branch, is concerned about the unanticipated high rates of injury from air bag deployment. The witness list for the hearings includes representatives of auto manufacturers, insurance companies, safety institutes, auto safety advocacy groups, air bag manufacturers, and auto parts suppliers. The purpose of the hearings is to enable the board to make recommendations for improving air bag safety.

Based on the board's ensuing recommendations and its own investigations, the federal agency responsible for automotive safety regulations, the National Highway Traffic Safety Administration (NHTSA) announces that it intends to modify the current standard for air bags. The agency announces its proposed modification in the *Federal Register* and calls for public comment.

In response to the call for comments, two experts in automotive safety jointly write a technical comment (Example 1, this chapter) and submit it in the rule making process described in the scenario. They point out shortcomings in the agency's proposed modification, and they propose an alternative.

---

### Comment to The Docket Concerning Amendments to Fmvss 208, Occupant Crash Protection

#### Summary of Comments

Federal motor vehicle safety standards (FMVSS) must, by law, meet the need for motor vehicle safety. This proposal (Docket No. NHTSA 98–4405; Notice 1) purports to meet that need by requiring advanced air bags. In fact, it is primarily written to address the problem of inflation induced injuries and would provide little additional protection.

The worst of the inflation-induced injuries resulted in several hundred fatalities to children and out-of-position adults (including those sitting too close to the steering wheel) and from late, low-speed crash air bag deployments. NHTSA [National Highway Traffic Safety Administration] had assumed that manufacturers would conduct comprehensive air bag testing to ensure that inflation would not inflict injury under reasonable foreseeable conditions. It is arguable (although probably not practical policy) that NHTSA could address inflation-induced injuries under safety defect provisions of the National Traffic and Motor Vehicle Safety Act.

...

A key part of this notice proposes two options: (1) tests of air bag systems with dummies in close proximity to ensure that inflation induced injuries are unlikely, or (2) requirements for occupant sensors to ensure that air bags will not inflate if an occupant is in a position where he or she is at risk of injury from the inflating air bag.

In response to the proposed alternatives, we expect manufacturers to choose occupant sensors to prevent air bag inflation for certain occupant situations. This untested sensor technology might actually increase casualties because of inaccurate determinations of occupant risks and degraded reliability from the added complexity.

Experts in the field have suggested a number of potential air bag design and performance features that might reduce inflation induced injuries. The Canadian government and NHTSA deserve credit for their research and analysis in this field despite NHTSA's belated recognition that an official response was necessary. It is not clear which approach would be most effective, or even most cost-effective, but we think it is unlikely that NHTSA's proposed regulation will yield an optimal result.

This notice [of proposal amendments] also fails to address occupant protection challenges involving one to two orders of magnitude more casualties for which feasible technologies are available. These include raising safety belt use to near universality, protection of occupants in rollover crashes, and addressing compatibility problems between passenger cars and light trucks.

Many of these deficiencies can be overcome with a third alternative that retains the simplicity of the original automatic occupant crash protection standard; does not introduce complex, untested occupant sensors; and meets other needs for motor vehicle safety. It depends fundamentally on NHTSA's willingness to propose acceptable, effective inducements for using safety belts.

...

## A Third Option Would Encourage Belt Use

We are proposing that a third option be added to NHTSA's notice that would ensure safety belt use with acceptable and effective belt use inducements built into the vehicle.

...

NHTSA must recognize that the fundamental problem with its occupant restraint policy is that a substantial minority of motorists does not use safety belts. In fact, a much larger proportion of those most likely to be involved in serious crashes drive unbelted. Nearly universal belt use is critical to any rational occupant crash protection program.

...

## An Alternative to the Proposed Amendment

Our specific proposal is that NHTSA add a third option to its notice on advanced air bags. Under this option:

- A manufacturer must install an effective, but not onerous safety belt use inducement in a new motor vehicle of a type that would be permitted under the "interlock" amendment (15 U.S.C.1410b) to the National Traffic and Motor Vehicle Safety Act.

...

- A motor vehicle must meet comparative injury criteria of FMVSS 208 and in addition [in crashworthiness tests using dummies] there can be no contact between the head of the driver or passenger dummy and any part of the vehicle (other than the air bag or belt restraint system) or any other part of the dummy, in a frontal barrier crash at a speed of up to 35 mph with belted occupants

...

- Air bags may not deploy under any frontal crash speed barrier impacts below 16 mph.

...

## Discussion

Our alternative would provide occupant crash protection that is at least equal in all respects to that provided by the present standard and NCAP consumer information program.

...

This proposal would substantially increase belt use and, because of the head impact requirements, would ensure that air bags provide good head protection. Air bags that can meet this criterion would provide some frontal crash protection to the small number of unbelted occupants (who would, of course, be unbelted by their own conscious choice).

If manufacturers would choose our alternative, it would save a minimum of 7000 lives per year compared with the present FMVSS208, making it one of the most cost-effective standards ever.

(The full comment can be found at http://www.regulations.gov. See NHTSA 1999–6407–0073. It has as Appendix 1 the commenters' additional petition on the subject.)

Later, the NHTSA summarizes all comments received in a preamble to its next published notice on air bag safety, and says how the comments influenced its plans to modify the standard. The preamble states, "In response to the public comments on our 1998 proposal and to other new information obtained since issuing the proposal, we are issuing a supplemental proposal that updates and refines the amendments under consideration." In an appendix, NHTSA states its reasons for rejecting the two experts' proposed alternative.

## Example 2

### Scenario

A state environmental protection department's bureau of mining, which regulates mineral extraction industries in the state, announces a proposed revision in a mining company's operating permit. In accordance with "sunshine" requirements for permitting processes, the agency publishes the applicant's proposal to mine deeper than its original permit allowed. The mining company is asking the bureau to remove restrictions on the company's operation at a specific site. The primary restriction prohibits mining at levels that might adversely affect local groundwater quantity and quality. The restriction is warranted in a region where well-water supply and quality varies according to groundwater conditions and where high quality cold-water trout fishing streams are fed by local springs near the mining site.

In response to the bureau's call for public comment on the mine operator's request for permit revision, a local environmental conservation group and a local civic organization write letters of comment (Examples 2 and 3, this chapter). Other interested parties write letters, too, including a national sport fishing group, local businesses dependent on tourism, and individual citizens. At the request of the civic organization, the agency holds a public meeting. The conservation group hires a professional stenographer (who is also a notary public) to transcribe the meeting. In addition, the group invites local news reporters. The meeting is well attended. The bureau officials, the mine operator, and the residents of the region affected by the mine vigorously discuss the request to lift restrictions on the mine. After the meeting, the conservation group provides the transcript to the bureau as a written record of public comment. If administrative litigation regarding this permit ensues, the transcript will provide evidence.

Following the public meeting, an attorney member of the local environmental conservation group, in collaboration with members who are expert in hydrogeology and water quality engineering, writes a technical and legal analysis of the mining company's application for permit modifications. The chair of the group's relevant committee signs and submits the comment. Selections are given here.

## TECHNICAL ANALYSIS

July 29, 2001

Michael W. Smith
District Mining Manager
Pennsylvania Department of Environmental Protection
P.O. Box 209 Hawk Run, PA 16840–0209
VIA Hand Delivery

Re: Con-Stone, Inc's, June 7, 2001, application to revise permit #14920301

Dear Mr. Smith:

The Penns Valley Conservation Association (PVCA) has reviewed Con-Stone, Inc.'s, June 7, 2001, application to revise permit #14920301 to allow removal of the Valentine Limestone below the 1080' elevation. PVCA wishes to work cooperatively with Con-Stone and the Pennsylvania Department of Environmental Protection (DEP) to ensure that mining operations protect the watershed surrounding the

Aaronsburg Operation, including Elk and Pine Creeks [state-designated Exceptional Value (EV) stream] and Penns Creek [state-designated High-Quality (HQ) stream]. In that spirit of cooperation, and for protection of those streams, PVCA requests denial of Con-Stone's current application for the following reasons.

1. PVCA recommends retaining special conditions 1, 2, and 4 in Part B, Noncoal Surface Mining Permit No 14920301, Revised July 13, 1999, Special Conditions or Requirements. As District Mining Manager Michael W. Smith said in an August 27, 1999, letter to Con-Stone, "The mining limit of 1080 feet was originally established to keep mining activity out of the average seasonal low water table to minimize the potential for impacts to groundwater and to Spring S-26. We are not convinced that mining below 1080 feet can be accomplished without added risk of water impact."

   ...

2. To manage the risks of mining below the water table, the proposed amendment calls for phased mining with a progressively deeper penetration of the water table. However, there is a total lack of detail in the permit amendment regarding the specific steps to be taken in the phased mining process. There should be clear language in the permit that stipulates consecutive mining and reclamation and attaches some time schedule and methodology for data analysis and reporting prior to advancing to the next phase of mining.

3. In PVCA's original discussions with DEP, Mike Smith indicated that Con-Stone would have to develop a new infiltration basin system to dispose of the groundwater pumped from the quarry. The permit amendment is contrary to this position as it utilizes the infiltration galleries currently designated for storm water disposal. PVCA requests that separate infiltration systems covered by separate NPDES permits be developed for the storm water and groundwater pumped from the pit.

4. The materials contained in the permit amendment do not adequately describe the hydrogeologic conditions. An appropriately scaled map showing the current pit location, the water table configuration, the location of all boreholes, the sedimentation basin, and infiltration galleries should be prepared. Without water table contour mapping, it is impossible to address issues such as recirculation of the water pumped from the mine.

5. The May 7–10, 2001, pit pumping test performed by the mine operator provides little useful information regarding the extent of [potential loss of water supply] due to mining operations....If DEP is going to grant the requested amendment, PVCA requests a special condition that Con-Stone is responsible for replacing the water supply for any water losses that result from mining operations. ...

6. ...In the context of the EV protection of the watershed, a much more comprehensive modeling effort is warranted. "Ideal aquifer" calculations such as those used to calculate inflow to the pit are not applicable in this setting.

7. Monitoring should be expanded, again at Con-Stone's cost, to be more complete by including all biological and chemical monitoring required by DEP's water quality anti-degradation regulations and implementation guidelines.

...

10. The permit amendment submission does not appear to be signed and sealed by a licensed professional geologist.

11. PVCA believes Con-Stone must apply for a new or revised NPDES [National Pollution Discharge] permit for the proposed quarry dewatering activities.

...

13. PVCA does not believe that Con-Stone has complied with all necessary pre-permit requirements under DEP's water quality anti-degradation regulations and implementation guidelines....Further, the application has not sought review by local and county governments to ensure compatibility with applicable regulations, ordinances, and comprehensive plans and to allow government to identify local and regional environmental and economic issues that should be considered.

Sincerely,
J. Thomas Doman Chair,
Watershed Committee Member,
Board of Directors, PVCA

cc: Jeff Confer, Con-Stone, Inc.
Hon. Jake Corman, Pennsylvania Senate
Hon. Kerry Benninghoff, Pennsylvania
House of Representatives
Pennsylvania Trout Unlimited

In announcing its decision later, the agency says, "The many public comments the Department received regarding this application formed the basis for modifications to the permit revision and resulted in changes in [the mining company's] proposed mining plan." The bureau's decision is to allow deeper mining, but to require new modifications intended to protect groundwater conditions.

### Example 3
This is a letter by a citizens group requesting the public meeting described in the scenario given earlier.

### LETTER

July 16, 2001

Re: Application for amendment for Con-Stone mining permit #14920301, Aaronsburg Operation

District Mining Manager
Department of Environmental Protection
Bureau of Mining
Hawk Run District Office
PO Box 209 Hawk Run, PA 16840–0209

On behalf of the Aaronsburg Civic Club I am requesting a public conference on the proposed amendment to the above permit. Again this year, we are offering our facility, the Aaronsburg Civic Club Community Building, for that purpose. As you are aware last year's public meeting was well attended and provided an opportunity for residents to state their concerns and for Con-Stone and DEP to address them. This is as it should be in a free and democratic society.

I strongly urge you to hold a public meeting on the latest proposed permit revisions. Two concerns that have been brought to my attention are (1) the potential degradation of underground and surface water, and (2) mining on land previously designated for storage.

Please contact me to reserve our facility.

Sincerely yours,
Earl Weaver, President
Aaronsburg Civic Club

*Example 4*

### Scenario

In 2011 the Department of Agriculture (USDA) called for public comment on a proposed National Leafy Greens Marketing Agreement (Scenario 2, chapter 3; Example 3, chapter 7). The National Sustainable Agriculture Coalition (NSAC) responded in a comment outlining eleven reasons for opposing the Agreement. Two of the reasons are presented here.

July 28, 2011
Hearing Clerk
U.S. Department of Agriculture
1400 Independence Ave., SW
Room 1031-S
Washington, DC 20250–9200

Melissa Schmaedick
Marketing Order Administration Branch
Fruit and Vegetable Programs
Agricultural Marketing Service
U.S. Department of Agriculture
805 SW, Broadway
Suite 930
Portland, Oregon 97205

Submitted via: http://www.regulations.gov
Emailed to Melissa Schmaedick, Melissa.Schmaedick@ams.usda.gov

**Re: Proposed National Marketing Agreement Regulating Leafy Green Vegetables**

**Federal Register / Vol. 76, No. 83 / Friday, April 29, 2011, pp. 24292–24337**

**Doc. No. AO-FV-09-0138; AMS-FV-09-0029; FV09-970-1**

Dear Hearing Clerk and Ms. Schmaedick:

We are submitting this letter in response to the proposed National Leafy Greens Marketing Agreement (NLGMA).

The National Sustainable Agriculture Coalition (NSAC) is an alliance of grassroots farm and rural organizations that advocates for federal policy reform to advance the sustainability of agriculture, food systems, natural resources, and rural communities. Our vision of agriculture is one where a safe, nutritious, ample, and affordable food supply is produced by family farmers who make a decent living pursuing their trade, while protecting the environment, and contributing to the strength and stability of their communities. Many NSAC organizations include small and mid-size agricultural producers of leafy green vegetables.

NSAC strongly opposes the proposal and urges USDA to withdraw it for the following reasons.

**1. The Proposed NLGMA is Inconsistent with Statute and Should Therefore be Withdrawn.**

The Agricultural Marketing Agreement Act of 1937 establishes marketing orders and marketing agreements for the purpose of creating "orderly marketing conditions" in interstate commerce for the benefit of agricultural producers. In addition, consumers are to be protected from inordinately high prices, and marketing research and development may be provided for "as will be in the public interest." Finally, "orderly marketing conditions" and "an orderly flow" of supplies is to be fostered "in the interests of producers and consumers." (Agricultural Marketing Agreement Act of 1937, Section 2, Declaration of Policy)

An agreement proposed by handlers that is objected to by many farmers, farmer organizations, and consumer organizations should never have been cleared for publication as a proposed agreement. USDA is absolutely correct in labeling the proposal an "industry proposal" in its summaries of the NLGMA and as such the Department has overstepped its authority in moving a handler-initiated proposal as a proposed marketing agreement under the terms of a law which does not include industry handlers as a protected class. Giving industry leaders the authority, through effective control of the marketing agreement (see section 11 below), to administer a program that will effectively regulate their growers creates at the very least the appearance of insider abuse and manipulation. USDA should not be party to such an agreement and should have rejected it on that basis.

The proposed NLGMA not only serves the wrong constituency relative to the congressionally mandated purposes of the program, but it also does nothing to serve the overriding purpose of the statute to create orderly marketing conditions. In fact, quite to the contrary, it fosters more market disruption and confusion by introducing a new and potentially contradictory overlay to the Food Safety Modernization Act passed by Congress last year and signed into law by the President at the beginning of 2011. Proposing multiple regulations by multiple government agencies or government-sponsored entities on the same subject violates important "good government" principles. Having seen this would so clearly be the case as the Food Safety Modernization Act was becoming law, USDA should have rejected the proposed agreement instead of bringing it forward as a proposal in the Federal Register.

...

### 4. Food Safety Should be Pre-Competitive but this Proposed Agreement Threatens that Fundamental Core Principle and is Thus Dangerous and Unreasonable.

By adding food safety to its repertoire and by creating a marketing agreement for food safety, AMS would send an inherently biased message that marketing promotion and food safety are interconnected. Consumers should not be led to believe that by selecting products of a particular marketing agreement or brand that they are therefore purchasing "safer" foods.

The members of the National Sustainable Agriculture Coalition have issued a statement containing 16 core principles about food safety. The very first of those principles states:

**Food safety is noncompetitive and transparent.** Everyone who lifts a fork has a right to safe and healthy food, just as they have a right to choose foods based on the qualities most important to them. "Food safety" should not be a competitive marketing food-trait, lest the most vulnerable people end up with access to only the least safe food, or simply fewer choices. Every person has a right to expect the safest possible food, and a right to absolute transparency about its production processes, no matter what they can afford to pay for it. Completely open, public information about what makes a food "safe" is not negotiable.

Contrary to this principle, marketing agreements are designed to manage and promote the sales of products. It is an important purpose, but it is not a food safety purpose and it is fundamentally at odds with food safety principles....By making food safety a marketable attribute the NLGMA flies in the face of the pre-competitive principle.

According to the AMS summary of the NLGMA on its website, "A signatory handler's compliance with the program would be signified by the use of a program certification mark on producer and handler sales transaction and shipping paperwork (bills of lading, manifests, etc.)." In other words, meeting the food safety terms of the NLGMA would be communicated both by the farmer and by the handler as product moves through the supply chain. Handlers who do not participate in the agreement, and farmers who supply those handlers, as well as farmers who do not operate through handlers at all because they opt to use more direct marketing mechanisms, would be implicated by this system as subpar or out of compliance.

This is the very definition of a system that intends to use food safety as a marketing mechanism. This is an extremely dangerous road to go down…USDA should not start down this road and put one the most basic food safety principles at extreme risk.

(The full comment can be found at http://sustainableagricul ture.net/wp-content/uploads/2011/07/NSAC-Comments-on-the-NLGMA-Proposal-7–29-11.pdf.)

---

**✏ WHAT THESE EXAMPLES SHOW** All four examples exhibit qualities of effective public policy communication (Checklists, chapter 2). They illustrate useful public comments made from a variety of legitimate perspectives. They suggest a range of policy actors who exercise the right to comment on proposed government action.

In Example 1 on auto safety and Example 2 on stream water quality, experts show authority for their claims by invoked federal motor vehicle safety standards and state environmental protection regulations. In Example 3, concerned citizens invoke the authority of "sunshine" mandates for public participation in a state governmental decision affecting their town.

Examples 1 and 2 are technical. Although the contents are organized and subheadings are provided to aid comprehension, some of the details (test results, for example) might be moved to an appendix. However, the choice to use that option should depend on the writer's knowledge of the circumstances in which the documents will be read and used. Particularly, calls for comment might specify whether appendices can or cannot be provided. Generally, writers should be certain that all readers can access the entire document before deciding to move crucial details to an appendix.

Example 4 argues from a perspective of law and political philosophy. In the selections shown, the comment makes an argument based on values of upholding the intent of law and protecting public safety. (Other sections not shown here critique the technical provisions of the proposed agreement such as its governance structure.) The position taken in Example 4 supports a public interest approach and opposes a marketplace approach to safety policy. In documentation, Example 4 exhibits structural organization for coherent, clear, concise presentation. These features matter in public comments because many comments will be received. Well-organized comments might get more attention. Taken together, the four examples suggest the robust potential of the genre, formal public comment, for getting concerns on the public agenda and in the public record.

## Summary and Preview

It is surprising that few of us comment on action that government intends to take when the responsible agencies directly ask us to do so. This chapter aims to encourage and enable the practice of publicly commenting. Democratic self-governance depends on our willingness to intervene in the process. Concluding remarks, next, point to ways the Internet is increasing our capacity for intervention.

# Conclusion:
# Continuity and Change

## Key Concepts

- continuity
- change
- networked writing

Whenever public policy is made, communication will continue to be necessary and integral. Purposes will persist while processes will change. New communication media will emerge.

Genres introduced in this guide—defining policy problems, researching legislative history, arguing, petitioning, proposing, briefing, testifying, and commenting on proposed action—will continue, perhaps in altered forms. Cultural expectations will continue to value usefulness, clarity, credibility, and authority. In short, policy writers will continue to face demands for understanding the cultural context of policy making, and for applying their understanding and knowledge to communicate purposefully and ethically in the process.

What changes might you anticipate? Developments in communication technology will bring the greatest change. Recently, the Internet has emerged as an all-inclusive medium or the medium on which any information can be delivered to users. Owing to new network capabilities, information is no longer tied to a particular communication device. Content's form is no longer determined by its medium of delivery. For example, a telephone conversation does not require a telephone; the conversation might be conducted via the Internet. Similarly, radio or television broadcasts do not require a radio or television, and print documents do not require paper. Information created originally in any of those media may now be adaptively communicated, received, and used on the Internet through the World Wide Web interface. Or, information may originate and function entirely in the Internet environment.

What does the inclusive or all-media Internet mean for policy writers? The immediate, practical answer is that communicators must now choose how to use the Internet for their purposes. The choice is not whether to use the network, but how to use it.

To reflect more generally on the question, assume a framework of mixed continuity and change. As continuity, recall that people in policymaking roles will go on communicating in forms associated with their institution- or process-related roles (chapter 2). As change, reflect on recent historical changes of infrastructure that enabled new ways of communicating. For example, cellular wireless technology changed telephone use; now cell phones are changing computer use (Markoff 2009). In that frame of mixed continuity and change, bring the policy process into focus. Recall (from chapter 2) three categories of policy role-players: professionals inside government, professionals outside government, and active citizens.

Professionals who create and use information inside government will increasingly perform work via e-government, which means conducting jurisdictional responsibilities online (*Wikipedia*). Claimed benefits of e-government include better interoperability among agencies and greater transparency between government and citizens. Evidence suggests that the transparency benefit is real. In the United States, Internet users routinely access governmental information online rather than by other means. In 2003, the Pew Internet & American Life study reported "77% of American Internet users went online to search for information from government agencies or to communicate with them" (Allison and Williams 2008). Thus, professionals in government agencies now routinely provide information and interact with information users through websites. The sites are expected to meet prescribed standards for the electronic exchange of information (American National Standards Institute and the National Institute of Standards and Technology), as well as traditional standards for usefulness, clarity, credibility, and authority.

Beyond informing and interacting with the public, professionals in government and elected officeholders apply the Internet's capabilities to policymaking functions, too. Problem definition and policy analysis are examples. Sound, visualization, animation, and statistical modeling in "decision theaters" of integrative technologies enhance the representations of conditions, problems, and proposed solutions (Arizona State University Decision Theater).

For professionals outside government, the Internet provides new tools for creating knowledge to be used in policy design. Such tools include searchable databases, content management systems, and subscriber-only discussion groups that link to government websites. Experts use these tools collaboratively to draft reports for government use. For example, multinational teams of scientists now routinely collaborate on reports about climate change to inform governments globally. Nongovernmental institutions created specifically for this purpose include a treaty, the United Nations Framework Convention on Climate Change (UNFCCC) and a working group created jointly by the World Meteorological Organization and the United Nations, the Intergovernmental Panel on Climate Change (IPCC).

The Internet may hold the most potential for active citizens. The all-inclusive communication medium builds capacity for participation and intervention in governance. For example, Barack Obama's 2008 presidential campaign showed that the electorate could organize as a mega-interest group through Internet capabilities for email, text messaging, blogging, and social networking. Internet-enabled coalitions challenge the conventional wisdom that dispersed populations and single individuals cannot influence the policy process. Dairy farmers scattered across Pennsylvania who organized rapidly into groups via e-mail to achieve policy change (chapter 1) illustrate the power of networked individuals. Additionally, the Internet greatly expands the single individual's capacity to be informed about governance. If Google News can now search 4,500 global news sources continuously and deliver summaries personalized according to your ZIP code or your browsing pattern, might it someday search global government records databases and deliver multinational legislative histories on specified topics at your request?

Limits on change should be acknowledged. Cultural context, especially Internet access, is a limit. Geopolitical, economic, and infrastructure constraints determine who has Internet access. Now, access is not universal or evenly distributed. Latest statistics on Internet usage penetration in populations by world region show that penetration in North American regions is 78.3 percent, as compared with 30.2.percent worldwide and 11.5 percent in African regions, for example (Internet World Stats Usage and Population Statistics). In developed nations such as the United States, rural locales have uneven access or no access. It remains to be seen whether e-government will serve everyone equally well.

## Summary and Looking Forward

Public policy writers can look forward to continuity and to change, especially Internet-related change. As student, intern, professional, officeholder, or citizen, you might wish or you might be required to write in adapted or new Internet forms. When that happens, start by consulting the appendix on policy writing for the Web that follows next, here. There you will find this guide's know-how principles applied to networked communication along with resources for how-to skill development.

## References

Allison, L., and M. F. Williams. 2008. *Writing for the government*. New York: Pearson Longman.

American National Standards Institute (ANSI). http://www.ansi.org. Accessed March 10, 2012.

Arizona State University Decision Theater. http://decisiontheater.org. Accessed March 10, 2012.

"e-Government." *Wikipedia, the free encyclopedia.* http://en.wikipedia.org/wiki/E-Government Accessed March 10, 2012.

Intergovernmental Panel on Climate Change (IPCC).http://www.ipcc.ch/ Accessed March 10, 2012.

Internet World Stats Usage and Population Statistics. http://www.internet worldstats.com/stats.htm. Accessed March 10, 2012.

Markoff, J. 2009. *The cellphone, navigating our lives*. NYTimes.com. 17 February.http://www.nytimes.com/2009/02/17/science/17map.html?page wanted=all

National Institute of Standards and Technology (NIST). http://www.nist.gov/index.html Accessed March 10, 2012.

United Nations Framework Convention on Climate Change. http://unfccc.int/2860.php Accessed March 10, 2012.

# Public Policy Writing
# for the Web

## Key Concept

- Adapting public policy information to the Web

In the 1980s with the gradual uptake of e-mail, chat, file or document transfer, and other text-processing applications, the Internet network became a means of everyday communication. In the mid-1990s the information-processing application World Wide Web pushed the Internet into the background where it became infrastructure. The popular Web interface, in effect, became the network. A new genre, the website, emerged to frame developments in online communication. Multimedia, connectivity, and interactivity became norms for content. In the early 2000s, integrated media and social networking again changed the norms for content, while cellular telephone technology widened network access. The practical lesson to draw from this history? Web-writing techniques change in tandem with an evolving communication technology and expanding global network. The best practice is to continue learning.

This appendix can help you intelligently adapt the craft of public policy writing to Web conditions. E-mail was previously discussed (chapter 8). Here, the public policy website is the focus. Emphasis is on writing clear text for sites. This appendix informs know-how by offering heuristics or conceptual tools for presenting public policy information on the Web. Resources for skill development in specific Web-writing practices are identified.

# Case

The Employee Free Choice Act, also known as the Card Check Bill, was passed by the House but not voted on in the Senate in 2008. It was reintroduced in 2009

> to amend the National Labor Relations Act to establish an efficient system to enable employees to form, join, or assist labor organizations, to provide for mandatory injunctions for unfair labor practices during organizing efforts, and for other purposes. (H.R.1409 and S. 560)

Big labor unions including the American Federation of Labor and Congress of Industrial Organizations (AFL-CIO), a voluntary federation of 56 national and international labor unions, pushed Congress to approve the legislation. The U.S. Chamber of Commerce, a federation representing three million businesses as well as state and local chambers, industry associations in the United States, and 112 American chambers in other countries, pushed Congress to oppose it.

The AFL-CIO (http://www.aflcio.org) and the U.S. Chamber (http://www.uschamber.com) used their websites for activism to create awareness and mobilize action. In activist terms, creation of awareness means communicating an interest in a problem or a position regarding it intentionally to persuade others to share the interest or agree with the position. Mobilization means organizing interested people to act or react to influence public policy.

In this case, the AFL-CIO and U.S. Chamber aggregated representations of the subject and capabilities for expressing opinion on their websites. Options included

- e-mail for action alerts or announcements calling on interested people to contact Congress members and newspaper editors using content provided in the alert ("canned" letters to legislators and "astroturf" to editors)
- podcasts or prerecorded audio material
- videos or prerecorded multimedia material
- blogs, shared online journals maintained by individuals or organizations for public posting
- wikis or collections of Web pages to which anyone with access can contribute or modify content

While debate continued, people interested in knowing the AFL-CIO's or the U.S. Chamber's position on the Employee Free Choice Act or in joining their advocacy could do so through links to these options on their websites. After debate and action, the content might or might not be accessible in archives linked to the website. That public record depends on voluntary organizational policies for retaining content.

**What this case shows.** The Web now serves as one of many competing platforms where policy agendas are enacted and policy work is conducted. The Web offers advantages of transmission speed, information delivery to local and global users, low publishing costs, and 24-hour access. In this case, the purpose was advocacy.

More broadly, this case illustrates now-common practices of integrating many communication options with websites, not only for advocacy purposes. Other nonprofit organizational and governmental websites show other purposes. Examples include

- documentation of policy analysis by publishing briefs and full texts of reports (The Cato Institute at http://www.cato.org and The Brookings Institution at http://www.brookings.edu)

- performance of administrative rule making by managing electronic submission of comments (http://regulations.gov)

- public engagement by civic discussion forums (http:// e-democracy.org)

Across the spectrum of policy work settings, writers need to learn practices of creating textual content for websites.

The Web alters writing practice, but it does not invalidate the standards for writing in the cultural context. Features of Web content must accommodate normative qualities of public policy information. For effectiveness, a Web communication must fit the culture of public policy making. Like much else in policy work, the fit might be messy. You are reintroduced to cultural expectations previously discussed (Checklists, chapter 2) and offered resources for thoughtfully adapting them to Web-writing conditions, below.

## Public Policy Communication Addresses a Specific Audience about a Specific Problem

The touchstones for communicating with actors in a policy process are your definition of a problem relative to others and your role relative to other actors' roles (chapter 3). Choices about Web use start with those touchstones. The complexity of public policy audiences, which involve multiple interests and diverse role players, calls for special consideration in content creation. Here's a good general principle for public policy Web communicators to follow: assume that Web communication is one-to-many, and learn all you can about your actual and potential audience(s).

Generally, Web-writing guides do not offer methods of complexity management and multidimensional audience analysis that are sufficient to meet the demands of public policy writing. A notable exception is the chapter on government websites in the specialized guide *Writing for the Government* (Allison and Williams 2008). If you are a government writer, another helpful source is HowTo.gov's "Knowing Your Audience and Doing Market Research" (http://www.howto.gov/web-content).

Try this heuristic for thinking about one-to-many public policy communication on the Web. Imagine a website as a public space, perhaps a forum, a marketplace, or a commons. The space contains varied people and kinds of stuff. In this public space, people are freely coming and going, noticing some people or stuff but ignoring others, pausing to talk or hurrying on, pausing to look at an object or rushing by, putting stuff in and taking stuff out of baskets, and so forth. Now, picture the people as actors or role players in the policy process of concern to you. The objects are bits of your intended content.

Look closer at the scene. What's happening? What types of actors or role players are present? Why are they here? Who's doing what? What abilities do they have? Do all have the same abilities? Which actors are putting bits in their baskets? Which bits? What do you want the actors to do with the bits?

When you know your purpose, whether it is advocacy, analysis, public engagement, or another intention, conceive your audience(s) to anticipate their need(s), purpose(s), and actions of engaging the content. Narrative and dramatic imagination aids the practice of information design for Web users. Information design is the skill of preparing information so that people can use it efficiently and effectively.

To translate this scene to an information design for a public policy website, work from the assumptions that

- a site has multiple users who have diverse purposes
- a site has multiple components of content expressed in varied information types
- components are organized into a site index or map of content for multiple users and diverse purposes
- a site has multiple functions
- functions are anticipated in a site navigation plan
- a site is planned as a whole before individual components are planned
- individual components are "chunked" or constructed with a focus local to that component
- individual components are explicitly labeled or captioned
- a site as a whole and individual components meet standards for usability including clarity and accessibility (discussed in more detail below)

## Public Policy Communication Has a Purpose Related to a Specific Policy Action

Each action in a policy cycle (Figure 1.1, chapter 1) requires information created by both governmental and nongovernmental actors (Viewpoint 1, chapter 2). For policy professionals in U.S. federal government, the institutional workplace significantly influences choices about Web use. Executive branch departments and agencies use the network extensively for informing and interacting with the public and for administrative functions. Presently, e-government (Conclusion) is practiced mostly by administrative departments, agencies, and offices of the executive branch. The legislative and judicial branches use the Web less. Congressional and Supreme Court offices use the Web primarily for public information and access to public records.

In government settings, accountability demands that a communication have an identifiable purpose that is disclosed. Nonprofit organizations and individual citizens have more latitude. For these actors, public disclosure and other aspects of accountability might be voluntary rather than obligatory. Writers who want more information on voluntary self-regulation might consult the guidance on public disclosure in "Principles for Good Governance and Ethical Practice" developed by Independent Sector, a nonpartisan coalition of nonprofit organizations (http://www.independentsector.org/panel/main.htm).

## Public Policy Communication Represents Authority Accurately

Credible policy communications identify their role in the policy process. Role identification shows the kind of power the communication represents. Roles may be evident in the presenting individual's or group's title (for example, Senator X or Office of the Governor) or by reference in the content (for example, Jane Y and other union members).

Also, a document's origination and, if appropriate, the writers' names should be identified. Contact information must be provided. These attributions give credibility because they enable verification. Writers who want to know more about credibility in Web communications might consult the research-based "Stanford Guidelines for Web Credibility" (http://credibility.stanford.edu/guidelines) developed by Stanford University's Persuasive Technology Lab (http://captology.stanford.edu).

## Public Policy Communications Use Appropriate Form and Content

Appropriateness of form starts with the writer's choice of a genre (Method, chapter 2). Genre choices in the Web environment require careful thought. As the case of AFL-CIO and U.S. Chamber of Commerce communication discussed earlier in this chapter shows, websites now creatively meld many communication functions and forms. Caution should accompany creativity, however. Options might be wasted if users cannot access them. Accessibility is discussed later in this Appendix.

Appropriate content choices start with the writer's purpose and the audience's purpose (Method, chapter 2). In the cultural context, rights and responsibilities are associated with information's creation and use. Generally, for nongovernmental policy actors in the United States, information is expression and free speech is a right with legal constraints. As illustration, see commentary on "Nonprofit Speech Rights" on the watchdog group OMBWatch's website (http://omb-watch.org). For actors in government, information is a public trust. More stringent legal constraints apply to government sources than to others. For illustration by one federal government executive department, see the U.S. Department of Agriculture's "Policies and Links," "FOIA" (Freedom of Information Act), and "Information Quality" in small print at the bottom of the department website's homepage (http://www.usda.gov/wps/portal/usdahome).

Writers who want to learn more about information rights and responsibilities in democracy, particularly about the freedom of information, might consult "Federal Open Government Guide" (http://www.rcfp.org/federal-open-government-guide) developed by the advocacy group The Reporters' Committee for Freedom of the Press (http://www.rcfp.org/foia).

## Public Policy Communication Is Designed for Use

Policy information is expected to be useful. In the cultural context of policy making, that means content that is relevant for a purpose and accountable (Method, chapter 2). Content is also expected to meet usability standards for public information including clarity and accessibility.

Clarity is associated with principles of "plain language" use in government and legal communications. Plain language use in U.S. federal government administrative agency documents was mandated by executive order in 1998. Recent legislation, the Plain Writing Act of 2009 (Senate Bill 574) and the Plain Language Act of 2009 (House of Representatives Bill 946), extended the mandate.

Communicators who want to know more about plain language use might consult *Federal Plain Language Guidelines*. These guidelines are produced and frequently updated by the Plain Language

Action and Information Network of U.S. (primarily federal) government employees. Links on this group's homepage (http://govfresh. com/tag/plain-language-action-and-information-network/) take you to resources for teaching, training, and learning. For a comprehensive list of resources, on the federal government website managers' guide HowTo.gov, see especially "Plain Language Writing for the Web" (http://www.howto.gov/web-content/manage/write-for-the-web). For additional private sector resources, see the Center for Plain Language (http://www.centerforplainlanguage.org). For Canadian and global resources, see The Plain Language Association International (http:// www.plainlanguagenetwork.org). For European Union and other national resources, see Clarity, an international organization of lawyers and interested lay people promoting plain legal language (http:// www.clarity-international.net).

Accessibility is associated primarily with making website content available to users with physical impairments or difficulty in seeing, hearing, or making precise movements; individuals with limited English proficiency; elderly users, and others with special needs. Also, accessibility includes serving a broad range of visitors to websites. Many people in the United States and elsewhere do not use advanced capabilities of the technology because they have lower connection speed, screen resolution, or browser limitations. The cost of network connection time may be a limiting factor, too.

Writers who want to learn more about making Web content accessible might consult the following guidelines developed by government agencies and the Internet community:

- U.S. Department of Justice Civil Rights Division "Accessibility of State and Local Government Web sites to People with Disabilities" at http://www.ada.gov/websites2.htm
- United States Access Board "Electronic and Information Technology Accessibility Standards (Section 508)" at http:// www.access-board.gov/sec508/standards.htm
- World Wide Web Consortium (W3C) "Web Content Accessibility Guidelines 2.0" at http://www.w3.org/TR/WCAG/
- Federal Web Managers Council "Provide Access for People with Disabilities (Section 508)" on HowTo.gov at http://www. howto.gov/web-content

## Summary and Looking Forward

From now on, public policy communicators' choice will likely be not whether to use the Web but, rather, how to use it. Know-how involves judgment. Discussion in this appendix informs judgment from historical and cultural perspectives. To develop skills in digital documentation, writers should learn by observing the evolution of communication on the Web. Practice updated Web-writing techniques recommended by general guides such as HowTo.gov (http://www.howto.gov) or specialty guides such as Stanford Guidelines for Web Credibility (http://credibility.stanford.edu/guidelines).

## References

Allison, L., and M. F. Williams. 2008. Government websites. *Writing for the government*, 153–202. New York: Pearson Longman.

U.S. House of Representatives. 111th Congress, 1st session. H.R. 946 *Plain Language Act of 2009*. ONLINE: http://thomas.loc.gov/cgi-bin/query/z?c111:H.R.946

U.S. Senate. 111th Congress, 1st session. S. 574 *Plain Writing Act of 2009*. ONLINE: http://thomas.loc.gov/cgi-bin/query/z?c111:S.574

# Index